Anzeige aus dem Jahr 1973, S.p.A. Accessori e Articoli Sportivi

Anzeige aus dem Jahr 1974, S.p.A. Accessori e Articoli Sportivi

Anzeige aus dem Jahr 1984, Nolan Distributors Ltd. Orchard House

Im Jahr 1972, als zum letzten mal ein Mensch seinen Fuß auf die Mondoberfläche setzte, die Beatles mit „Let it be" große Erfolge feierten und die Motorradbranche in Europa zu boomen begann, fasste unser Firmengründer im italienischen Bergamo den Plan, eine neue Art von Motorradhelm zu entwickeln.
Seither sind 45 Jahre vergangen. Vieles hat sich verändert. Aber ihr habt es uns ermöglicht, unserer Philosophie treu zu bleiben – vielen Dank.

NOLAN, INDUSTRIAL MANUFACTURING IN ITALY SINCE 1972

Alle Infos zur Nolan- und X-lite Kollektion 2017 online: nolangroup.de   facebook.de/nolangroup

BMW R nineT Racer in Tokio

Racing isn't always just about speed and performance. It's also about fun and style, friendship and freedom. Japan's vintage racers are celebrating precisely this spirit of racing. In the metropolis of Tokyo, Joy Lewis meets customizer Daisuke Mukasa and his Curry Speed Club. She rides her R nineT Racer through the megacity and heads out to lonely mountain roads near Mount Fuji and a vintage motorcycle race at Fuji Speedway.

Beim Racing geht es nicht immer nur um Geschwindigkeit und Performance. Es geht auch um Spaß und um Style. Um Freundschaft und um Freiheit. Die Vintage-Rennfahrer Japans zelebrieren genau diesen Spirit of Racing. In der Millionenmetropole Tokio lernt Joy Lewis den Customizer Daisuke Mukasa und seinen Curry Speed Club kennen. Mit der R nineT Racer geht es quer durch die Megacity, raus auf einsame Bergstraßen am Mount Fuji und zum Vintage Rennen auf den Fuji Speedway.

This photo cost $8,889.78 to make, which I'm fairly certain makes it the most expensive advertisement See See has ever ran. It involved separating my shoulder, a broken left humerus, shattered humerus head, 1 metal plate, 14 screws and 2 slices of pizza the nurses wouldn't let me eat. It went down something like this: Thor lent me his extra KTM and took me out for a little trail riding at a local area just a few miles outside the city limits of Portland, Oregon. Motorcycles have always been in my life, my dad was a pretty good racer in his day, and I have ridden all kinds of bikes on a variety of terrains over the years. I figured this would be no different. Both the KTM and the trail system was unforgiving, lots of hills, slick stumps and rolly rocks for my out of shape body. At about mile 16, not 45 minutes after we took this photo, I hit something that kicked me over the bars, forcing my hand to hit the gas with the full onion. What happened after that is only for the birds to describe, because I don't remember a thing. The kicker was it was 2 turns away from coming out of the woods back to the van. But hey... at least we got the shot!

THOR DRAKE

PHOTO & STORY: DUSTIN AKSLAND. SEE SEE MOTOR COFFEE CO HAS TWO LOCATIONS IN THE WESTERN U.S. PORTLAND, ORE & RENO, NEV. ONLINE AT SEESEEMOTORCYCLES.COM

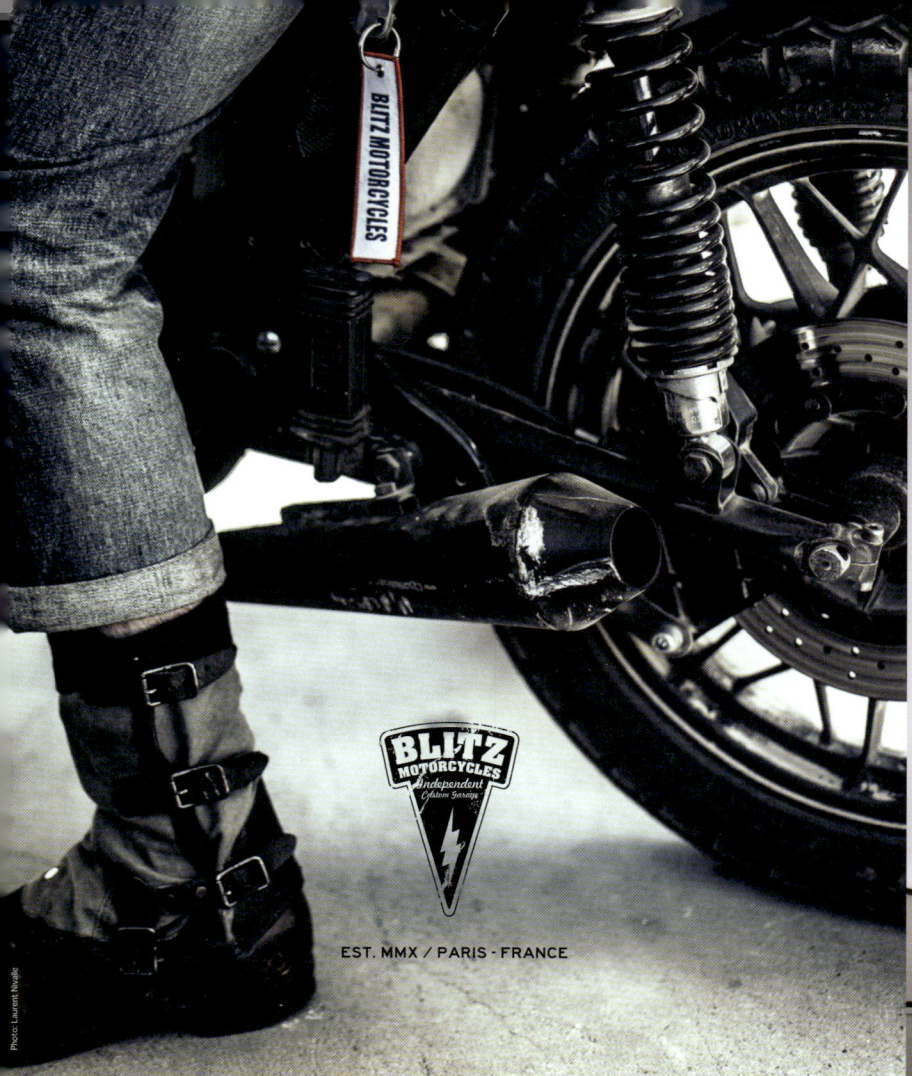

BLITZ MOTORCYCLES
BLITZ MOTORCYCLES
Independent
Custom Garage
EST. MMX / PARIS - FRANCE
Photo: Laurent Nivalle

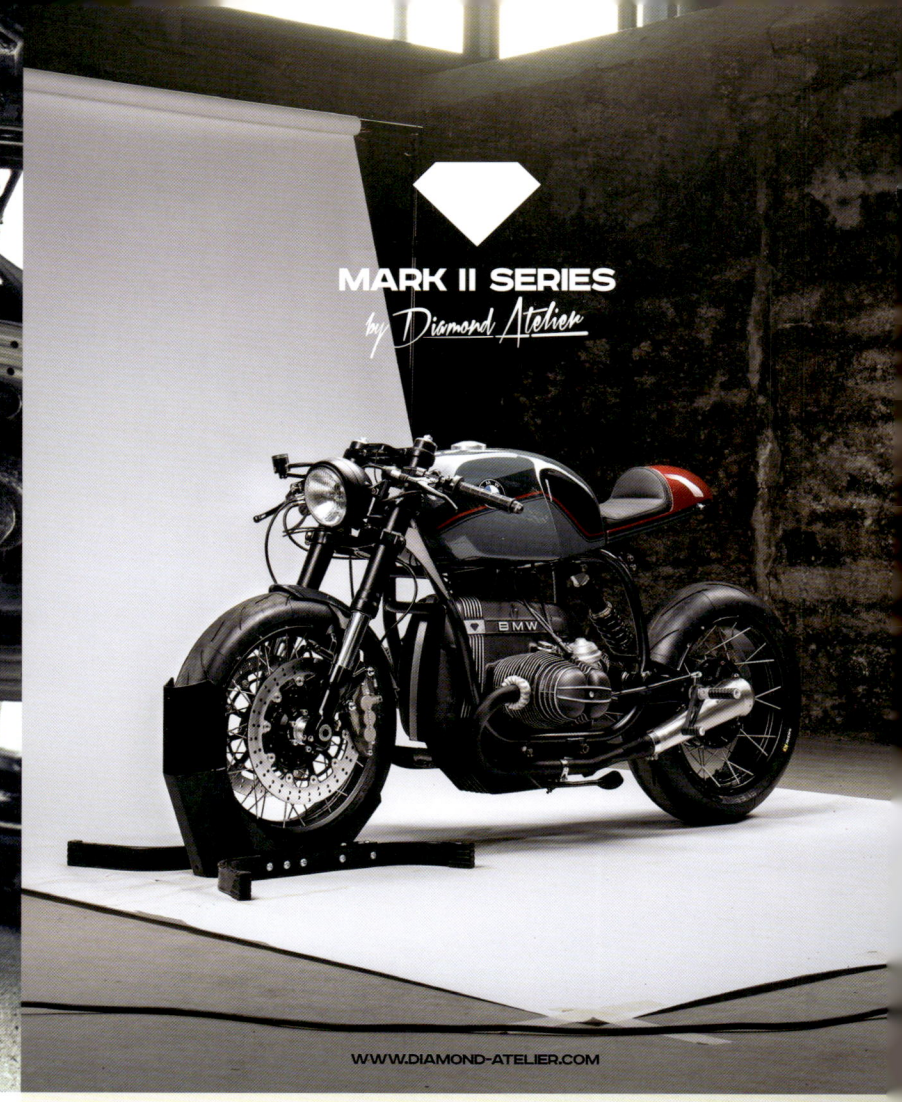

MARK II SERIES
by Diamond Atelier
BMW
WWW.DIAMOND-ATELIER.COM

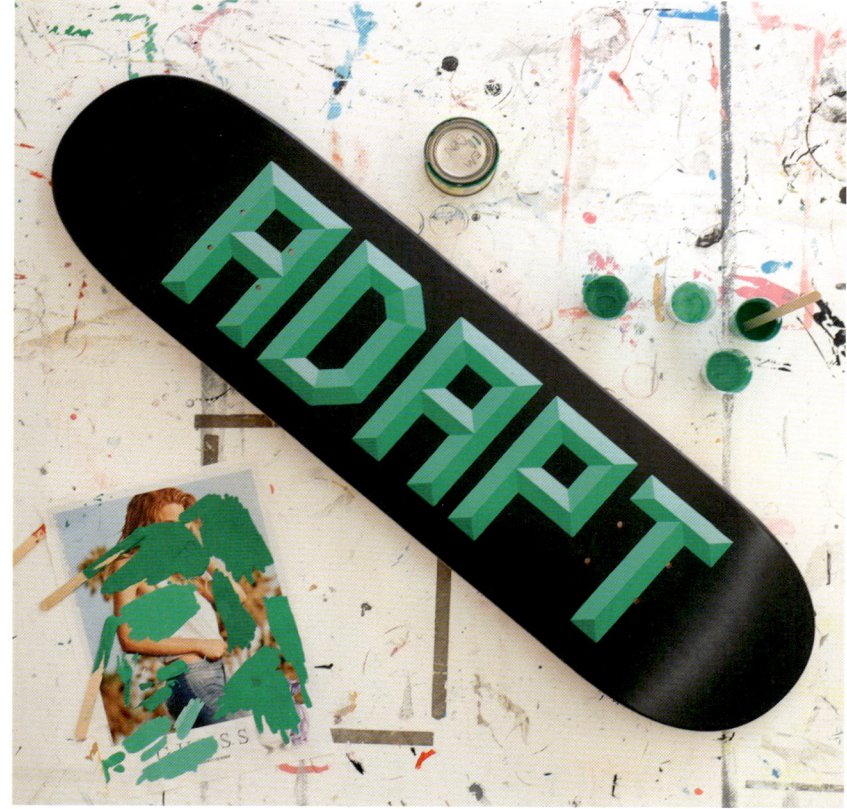

ADAPT
ORNAMENTAL
Conifer
Los Angeles

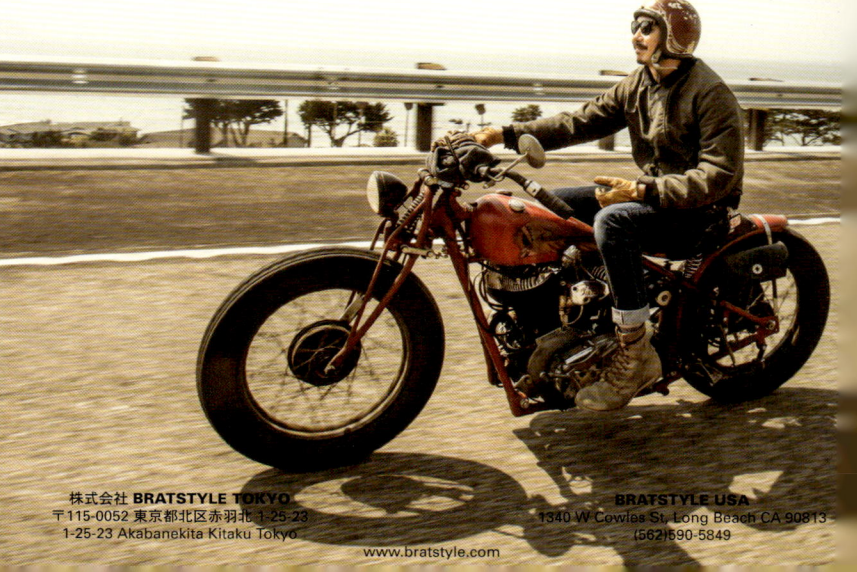

SINCE 1998
BRAT STYLE
TOKYO//CALIF
Be First Be Cool
株式会社 BRATSTYLE TOKYO
〒115-0052 東京都北区赤羽北 1-25-23
1-25-23 Akabanekita Kitaku Tokyo
BRATSTYLE USA
1340 W Cowles St, Long Beach CA 90813
(562)590-5849
www.bratstyle.com
Photo: Travis Shinn

BRITISH ONLY AUSTRIA
SPECIALIST IN ENGLISH SPARE PARTS

The specialist for
BROUGH SUPERIOR | VINCENT | VELOCETTE

Huge stocks of
TRIUMPH | BSA | NORTON spares

Also spares for
AJS | MATCHLESS | ARIEL | AMAL | LUCAS | CHAMPION | BOYER

400 different nuts | 500 different bolts | 250 different screws | 2000 used spares
We only sell what is in stock. Every part you see on our website is available NOW

You pay today – we ship today!

www.vintage-motorcycle.com

Photo by Matt Hind
www.matthind.com

British Only Austria Fahrzeughandel GmbH
Puehret 1 • A-4643 Pettenbach • Tel.: +43 7586 74 46 10 • www.vintage-motorcycle.com

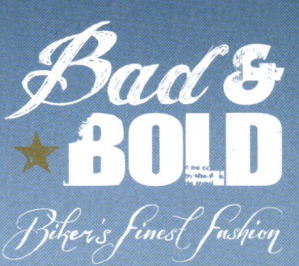

Bad & Bold
Biker's finest fashion

WWW.BADANDBOLD.COM

Picture powered by Temple Choppers, Munich.

BRUMM
ブゥオオオッ

Motorious Chronicles

Kristina Fender | Dimitri Coste | Larry Niehues | Paul d'Orléans | Hiro Maeda | James Tyler Reed
Mick Woollett | Ferruccio Testi | Cédric Dubus | Gary Margerum | Polo Garat | Raffaele Paolucci
Axel Borchardt | Alberto García-Alix | Vincent Prat | Christian Eusterhus | Hermann Köpf

WWW.BRUMMM.COM

	Images	Postscript

America
アメリカ
Larry Niehues
16 178

Classic Trials
クラシック トライアル
Hiroyuki Maeda
32 178

Cannonball 2016
キャノンボール
Susan McLaughlin & Paul d'Orléans
48 180

Flat Track Racing
フラットトラック レーシング
James Tyler Reed
64 181

Babes Ride Out
ベイブス ライド アウト
Kristina Fender
80 182

Trackracer Meeting
トラックレーサー ミーティング
Christian Eusterhus
96 184

Imola 1972
イモラ
Mick Woollett (1930–2014)
112 186

Focus
フォーカス
Dimitri Coste
128 187

Giro Motociclistico d´Italia 1923
ジロ モトチクリスティコ ディ イタリア
Ferruccio Testi (1882–1958)
144 188

HPN, Seibersdorf
エイチ ピー エヌ、ザイバースドルフ
Hermann Köpf
160 189

America
アメリカ

Larry Niehues

On the way to Matt's birthday, California 2013

Huggy, Los Angeles/CA 2014

Dan Collins, California 2013

Alboy, Redlands/CA 2016

Steven Johnson, Joshua Tree/CA 2015

Arizona 2013

Nevada 2015

Yoaii Hermelin, Lancaster/CA 2013

Luna, Angeles Crest 2015

Idaho 2015

Sur la route de Memphis, Tennessee 2015

Classic Trials
クラシック トライアル

Hiroyuki Maeda

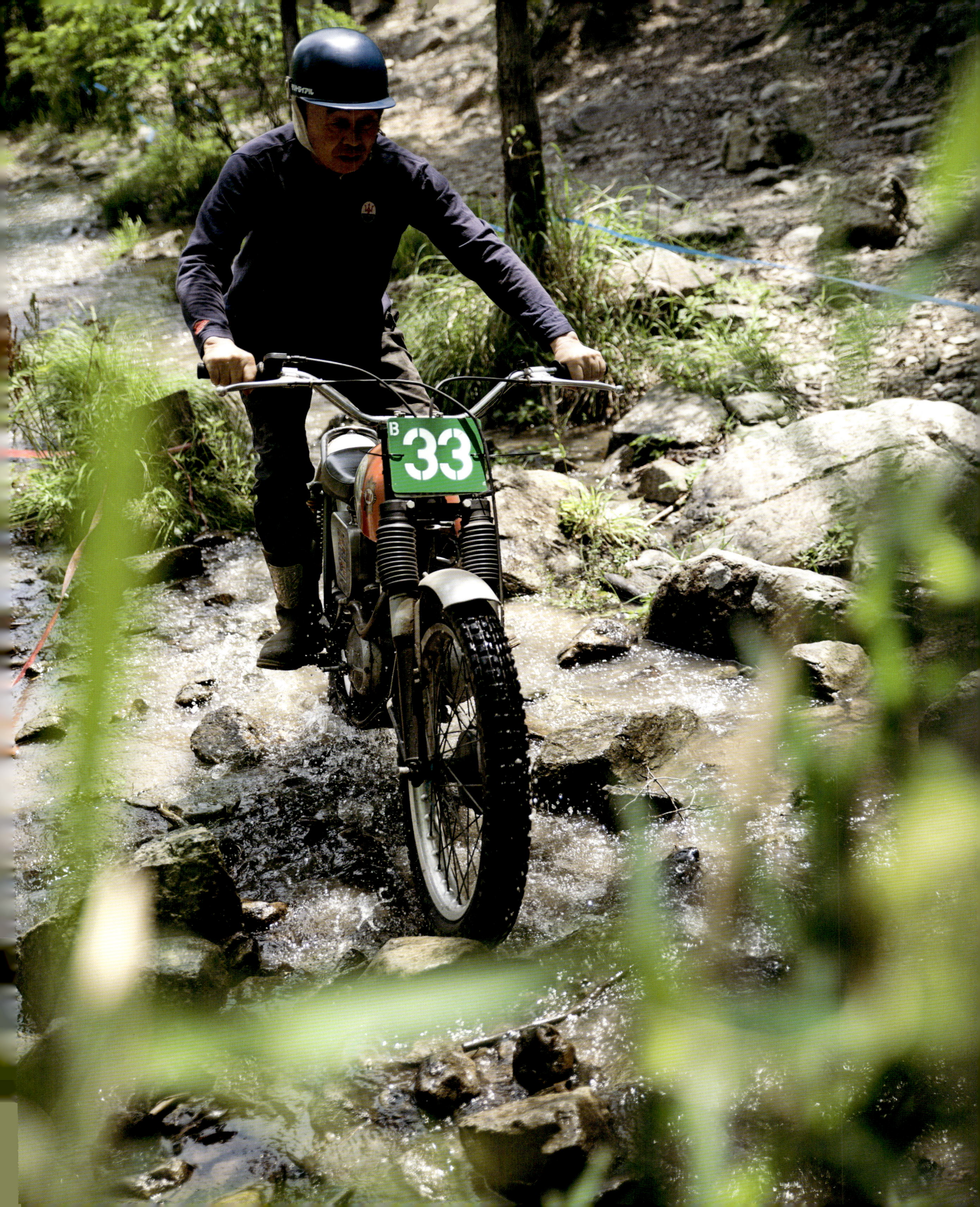
B 33

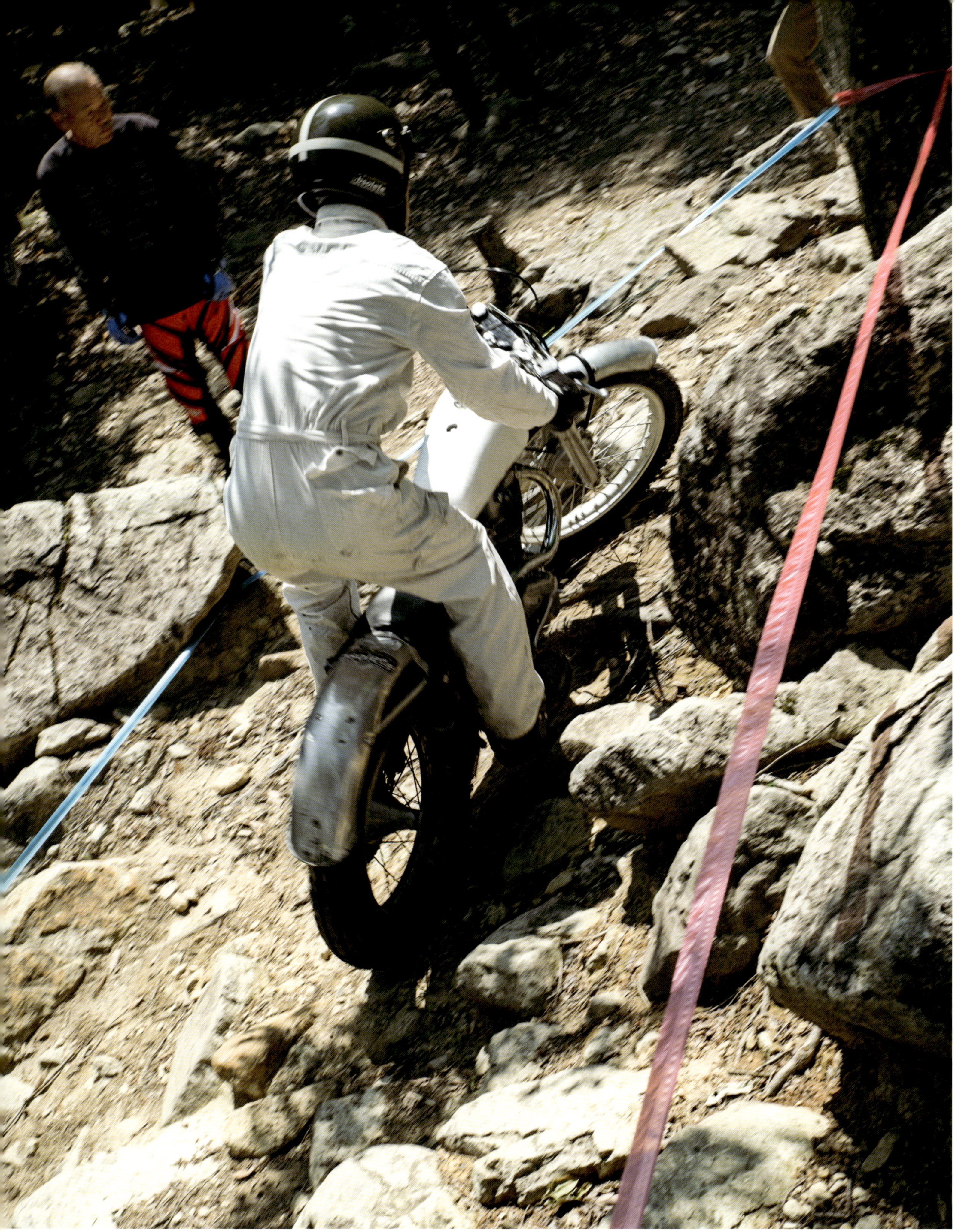

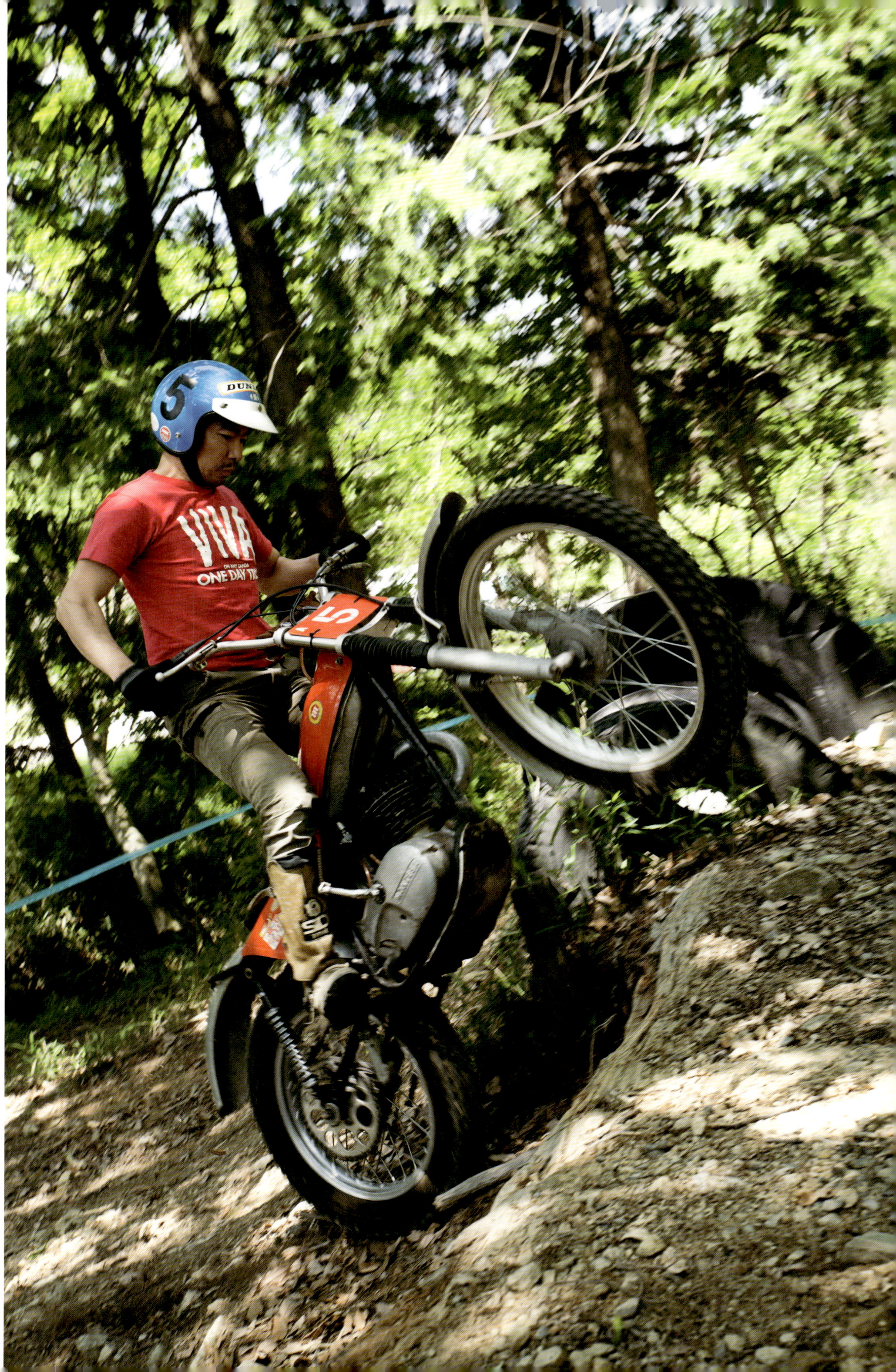
VIVA
ONE DAY TR
5

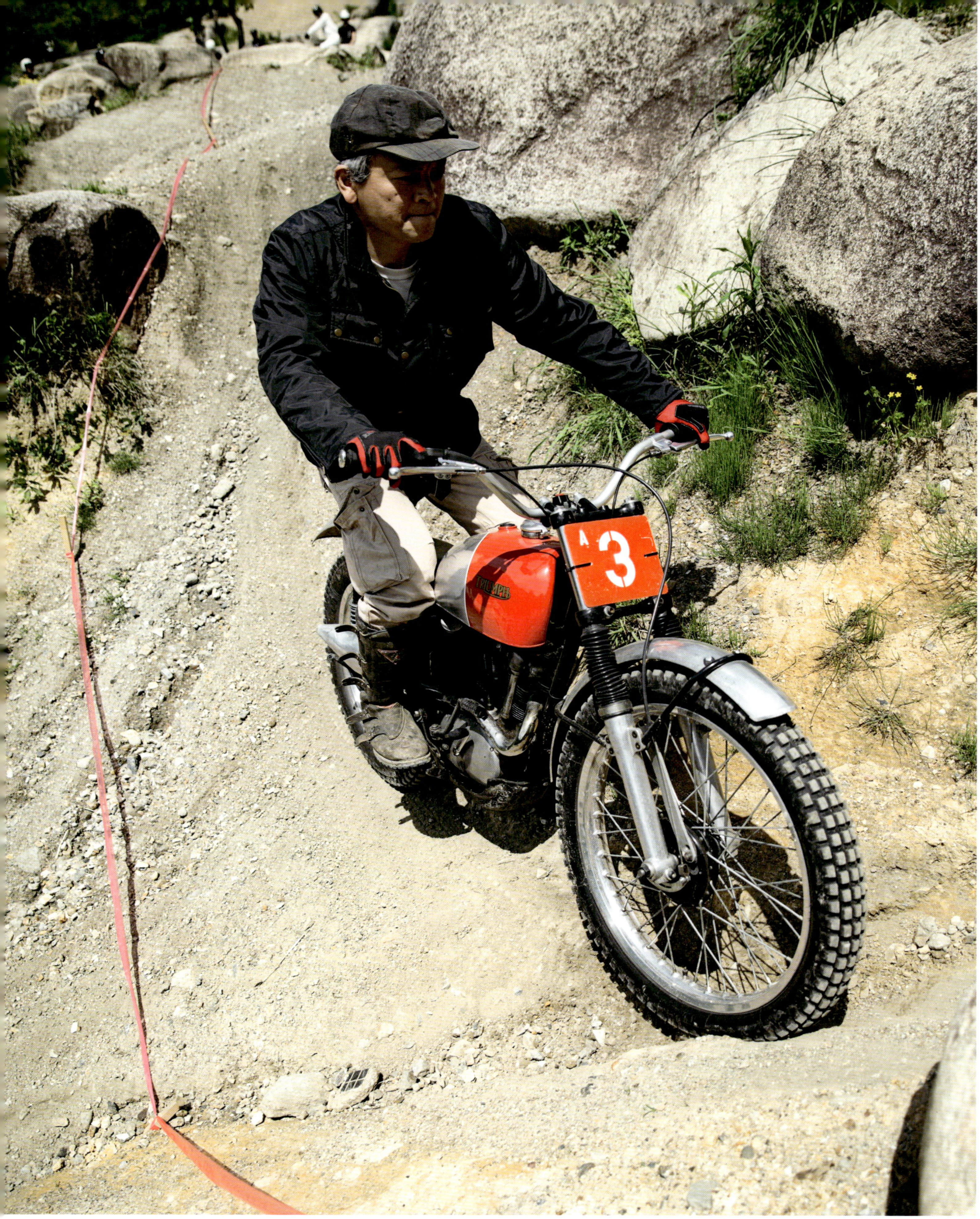
3

Sean Duggan with the 1915 Harley-Davidson bob-job he and Craig Jackman built for Bill Buckingham to ride in 2016. Bill was killed on his chopper in LA, two weeks before the 2016 Cannonball; Sean and Craig brought the bike to Colorado as a tribute to their great friend. Bill's Cannonball #40 was retired. (Alamosa, Colorado)

Sean Duggan mit der 1915er Harley-Davidson Bobber, die er und Craig Jackman für Bill Buckingham und sein 2016er Rennen gebaut haben. Bill starb bei einem Unfall mit seinem Chopper in LA zwei Wochen vor dem 2016er Cannonball Rennen. Sean und Craig brachten die Maschine zum Gedenken an ihren großen Freund nach Colorado. Bills letzter Cannonball #40. (Alamosa, Colorado)

Anthony Rutledge messing around on his 1915
Harley-Davidson, on the *day off* mid-Cannonball, at
Dodge City, Kansas. This train sits at Boot Hill, the
notorious Wild West site of Wyatt Earp's gun battles,
and the location of the *Gunsmoke* TV series.

*Anthony Rutledge albert am freien Tag der Halbzeit
des Cannonball Rennens in Dodge City, Kansas, auf
seiner 1915er Harley-Davidson herum. Der Zug steht
am Boot Hill, dem berühmten Platz, an dem Wyatt
Earps Schießereien stattfanden und der Ort, an dem
die TV Serie* Rauchende Colts *gedreht wurde.*

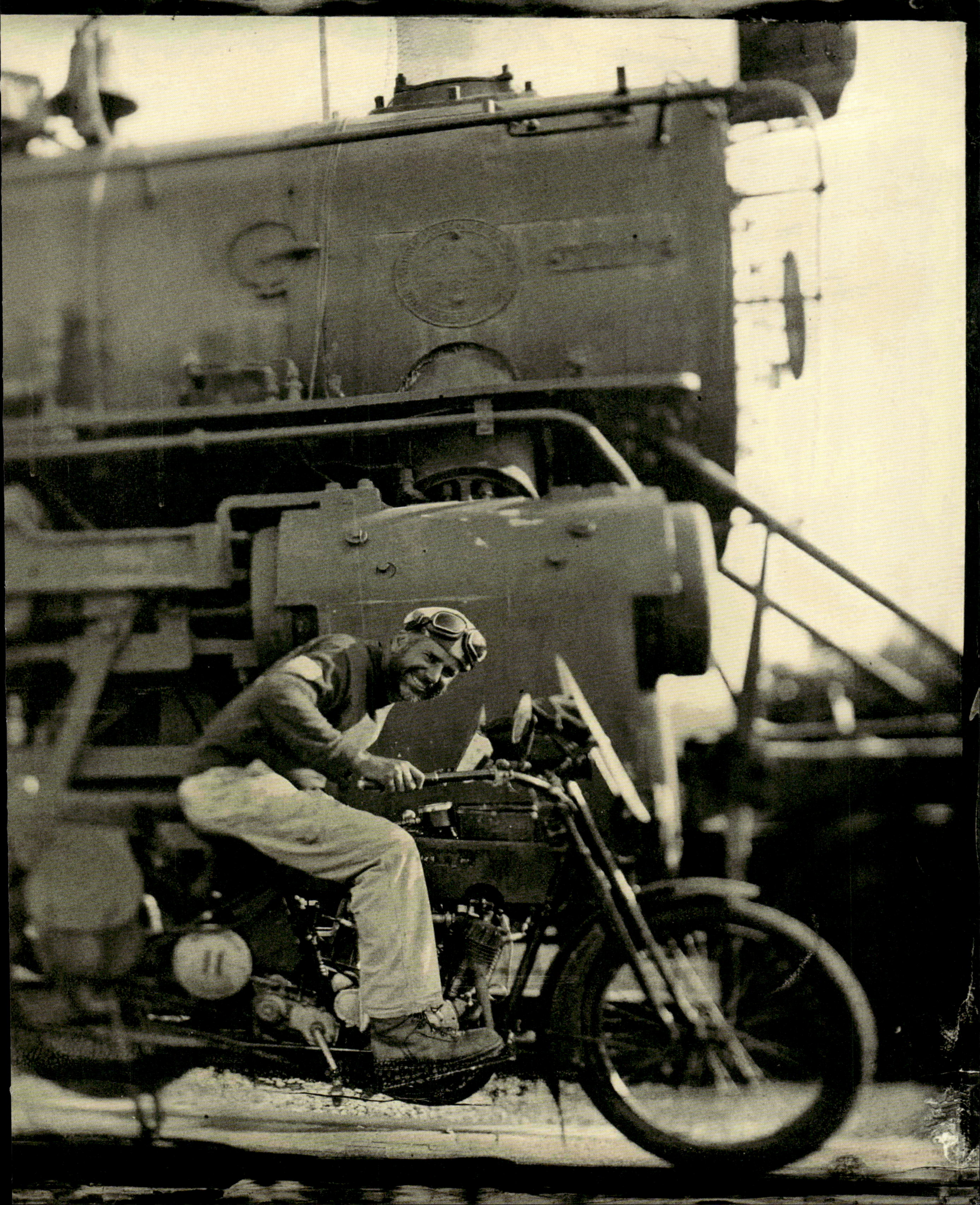
11

Dave Volnek, a veteran of three Cannonballs, here with his 1913 Indian. Dave's mysterious affect makes him a favorite portrait subject for our Cannonball studies. (Lake Havasu, Arizona)

Dave Volnek, bereits dreifacher Cannonball Teilnehmer, hier mit seiner 1913er Indian. Daves geheimnisvolles Aussehen machte ihn zum begehrten Fotoobjekt für unsere Cannonball Studien. (Lake Havasu, Arizona)

Norm Nelson and his 1911 Reading-Standard single. There were hundreds of motorcycle brands in the US before 1930, and Reading-Standard, of Reading Pennsylvania, was the first to use a sidevalve motor, in singles and v-twins. They're incredibly rare today. (Wichita, Kansas)

Norm Nelson und seine 1911er Reading-Standard Single. Vor 1930 gab es hunderte Motorradmarken in den USA und Reading-Standard aus Reading Pennsylvania waren die Ersten, die einen seitengesteuerten Motor, sowohl in einzylindrige als auch zweizylindrige V-Maschinen einbauten. Heute sind sie unglaublich selten. (Wichita, Kansas)

Linda Monahan with her 1914 Indian. In 2016, only 3 women entered the competition, although several more rode support motorcycles. Linda was the only woman rider attempting a solo crossing, with no backup team. Her Indian gave trouble, but she persevered. (Lake Havasu, Arizona)

Linda Monahan mit ihrer 1914er Indian. 2016 nahmen nur drei Frauen im Wettbewerb teil, obwohl einige mehr auf Begleitmotorrädern mitfuhren. Linda war die einzige Fahrerin, die eine solo Überquerung ohne Begleitteam versuchte. Ihre Indian machte Ärger, aber sie hielt durch. (Lake Havasu, Arizona)

Jared and Justin Rinker, identical twins on near-identical 1916 Indians, who rode with their father Steve on his '16 Indian. Their grandfather Buck was the team mechanic; a unique 3-generation Cannonball entry. (Alamosa, Colorado)

Jared und Justin Rinker, eineiige Zwillinge auf fast identischen 1916er Indians, die zusammen mit ihrem Vater Steve auf seiner 16er Indian fuhren. Ihr Großvater Buck war der Mechaniker des Teams – ein einzigartiger drei Generationen Auftritt. (Alamosa, Colorado)

Yoshimasa Niimi has traveled from Japan 4 times to share the Cannonball with his friend Shinya Kimura. Their 1915 Indian has never made every mile, and every night they work tirelessly to keep the ancient machine running sweetly. Usually it does, but not always; the Cannonball schedule is cruel. (Darlington, Pennsylvania)

Yoshimasa Niimi ist bereits vier Mal aus Japan angereist, um seinen Freund Shinya Kimura bei den Cannonball Rennen zu begleiten. Ihre 1915er Indian hat es noch nie bis zur Ziellinie geschafft und jede Nacht arbeiten sie unermüdlich daran, die alte Maschine zum Laufen zu bringen. Normalerweise tut sie das auch, aber nicht immer. Der Cannonball Zeitplan ist gnadenlos. (Darlington, Pennsylvania)

Shinya Kimura and his 1915 Indian, the only rider to use the same motorcycle in four Cannonballs. Watching his team (his wife Ayu and friend Niimi) nightly labor over the fragile Indian is silent poetry, accompanied by the quiet clink of tools, and occasional whispers in Japanese. (Williams, Arizona)

Shinya Kimura und seine 1915er Indian, der einzige Fahrer, der das gleiche Motorrad in vier verschiedenen Cannonballs fuhr. Seinem Team (Ehefrau Ayu und Freund Niimi) zuzusehen, wie sie jede Nacht an der empfindlichen Indian arbeiten, ist leise Poesie, begleitet nur von dem Klicken der Werkzeuge und gelegentlichem Flüstern auf japanisch. (Williams, Arizona)

Rick Salisbury and his 1916 Excelsior, and yet another steam train, this time at a lunch stop in Del Norte, Colorado. Rick owns the Legends Motorcycle Museum in Springville, Utah, and 2016 was his 3rd Cannonball.

Rick Salisbury mit seiner 1916er Excelsior und wieder einer Dampflok, diesmal während der Mittagspause in Del Norte, Colorado. Rick ist Besitzer des Legends Motorcycle Museums in Springville, Utah. 2016 war sein drittes Cannonball Rennen.

A border sign near Coolidge, Kansas. Colorado is not so colorful on the edge of the Great Plains. The Arkansas River nearby formed the border between Mexico and the *unorganized* northern Louisiana territory, purchased from Napoleon in 1803. You can see and feel history here; the trails where wagons crossed the plains heading westward, the rustic shacks of the settlers, the dismal reservations of the Native Americans, and suddenly, every town has a Spanish name. Crossing America slowly, on small roads, is an education on the country's past and present; it's all here to see. The near-abandoned but formerly rich towns by the Mississippi River, the stagnation in rural areas, the abandoned factories of the Rust Belt, the heavy tourism and relative prosperity in the West. But every mile was beautiful, the landscape changed daily, and we were always excited to see *what's next* in this great adventure across the USA.

Eine Grenzmarkierung nahe Coolidge in Kansas. Am Rande der Great Plains sieht Colorado nicht sehr farbig aus. Der nahe Arkansas River hat die Grenze zwischen Mexiko und dem unorganisierten *nördlichen Gebiet von Louisiana, 1803 von Napoleon gekauft, geformt. Hier sieht und fühlt man Geschichte: Die Spuren der Wagentrecks, die westwärts zogen, die alten Hütten der Siedler, die trostlosen Reservate der amerikanischen Ureinwohner und plötzlich hatte jede Stadt einen spanischen Namen. Die langsame Durchquerung Amerikas auf kleinen Straßen ist wie eine Lehrstunde über die Vergangenheit und Gegenwart des Landes, alles kann man hier sehen. Fast verlassene, ehemals reiche Städte am Mississippi, die stagnierende Entwicklung der ländlichen Gegenden, leerstehende Fabriken im Rust Belt, der starke Tourismus und relative Wohlstand des Westens. Aber jede Meile davon war schön, die Landschaften änderten sich täglich und wir waren immer gespannt darauf, was als nächstes passiert in diesem großen Abenteuer auf der Reise quer durch die USA.*

Flat Track Racing
フラットトラック レーシング

James Tyler Reed

Jeffrey Carver Jr.

Bronson Baumann

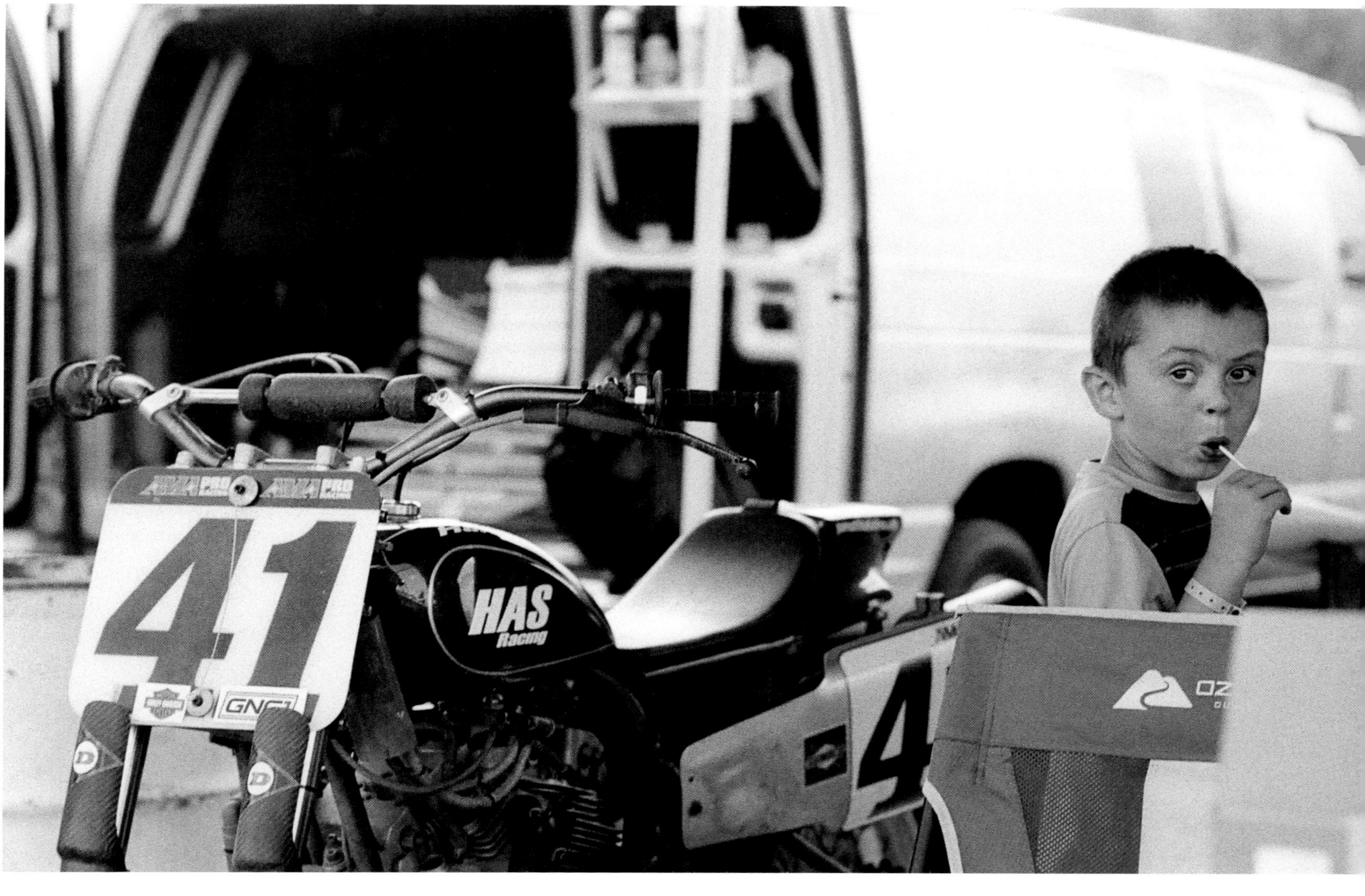
41
HAS
Racing
GNC

The guts of a GNC1 machine

Bryan Smith's Crosley/Howerton Kawasaki

Adjustments being made to Kenny Coolbeths's XR-750

MOTOR
HARLEY-DAVIDSON
CYCLES
6
HARLEY-DAVIDSON
GATOR
HARLEY-DAVIDSON
2
27
44

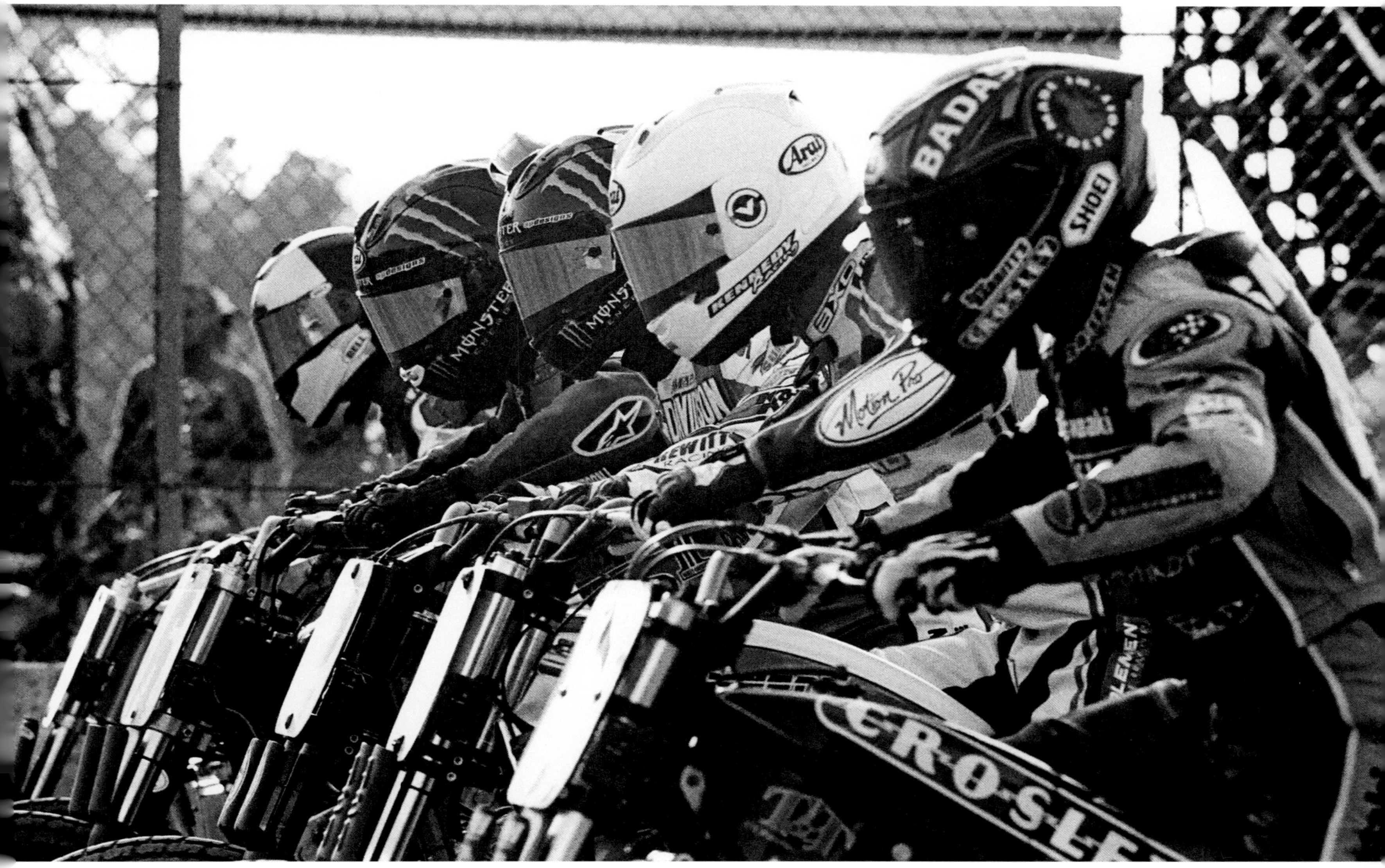
Arai
SHOEI
Motion Pro

Henry Wiles

Danny Eslick

Sammy Halbert

72/73

Brandon Wilhelm

One of the worst places to go down – Jake Mataya gets tangled up on the start line
Einer der schlechtesten Stellen für einen Sturz – Jake Mataya an der Startlinie

After a failed bump start attempt Jay Maloney pushes his bike back to the pits
Nach vergeblichen Anschieben, bringt Jay Maloney seine Maschine zurück in das Fahrerlager

19-year old Davis Fisher

Nick Armstrong

Ryan Foster

Baker
RACING
23

phMotorcycles.com
Castrol
TRIUMPH
Motion Pro
Quality Tools and Controls

78 / 79

Babes Ride Out
ベイブス ライド アウト

Kristina Fender

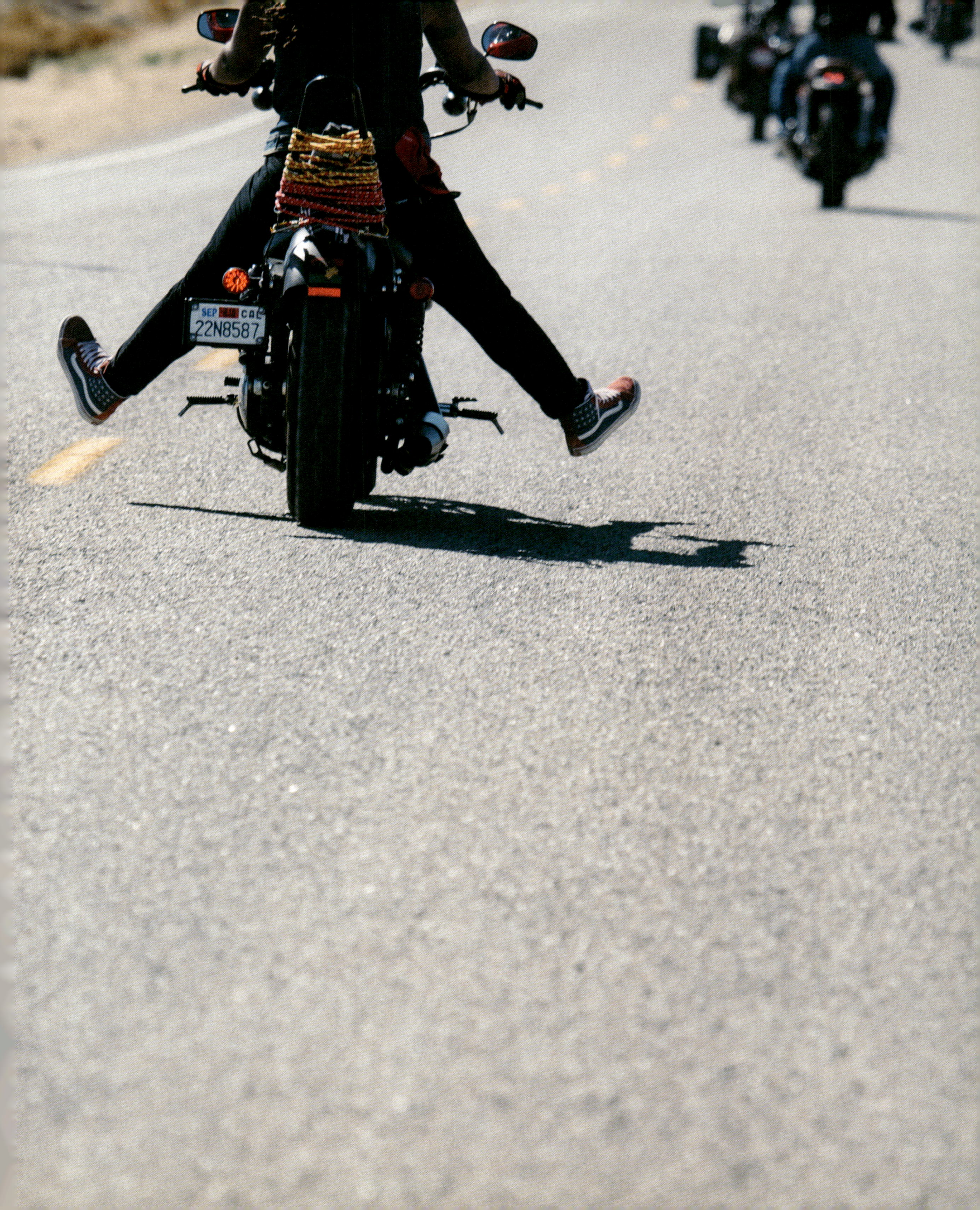
22N8587

Stacie B. London's *(Triple Nickle 555)* crew.

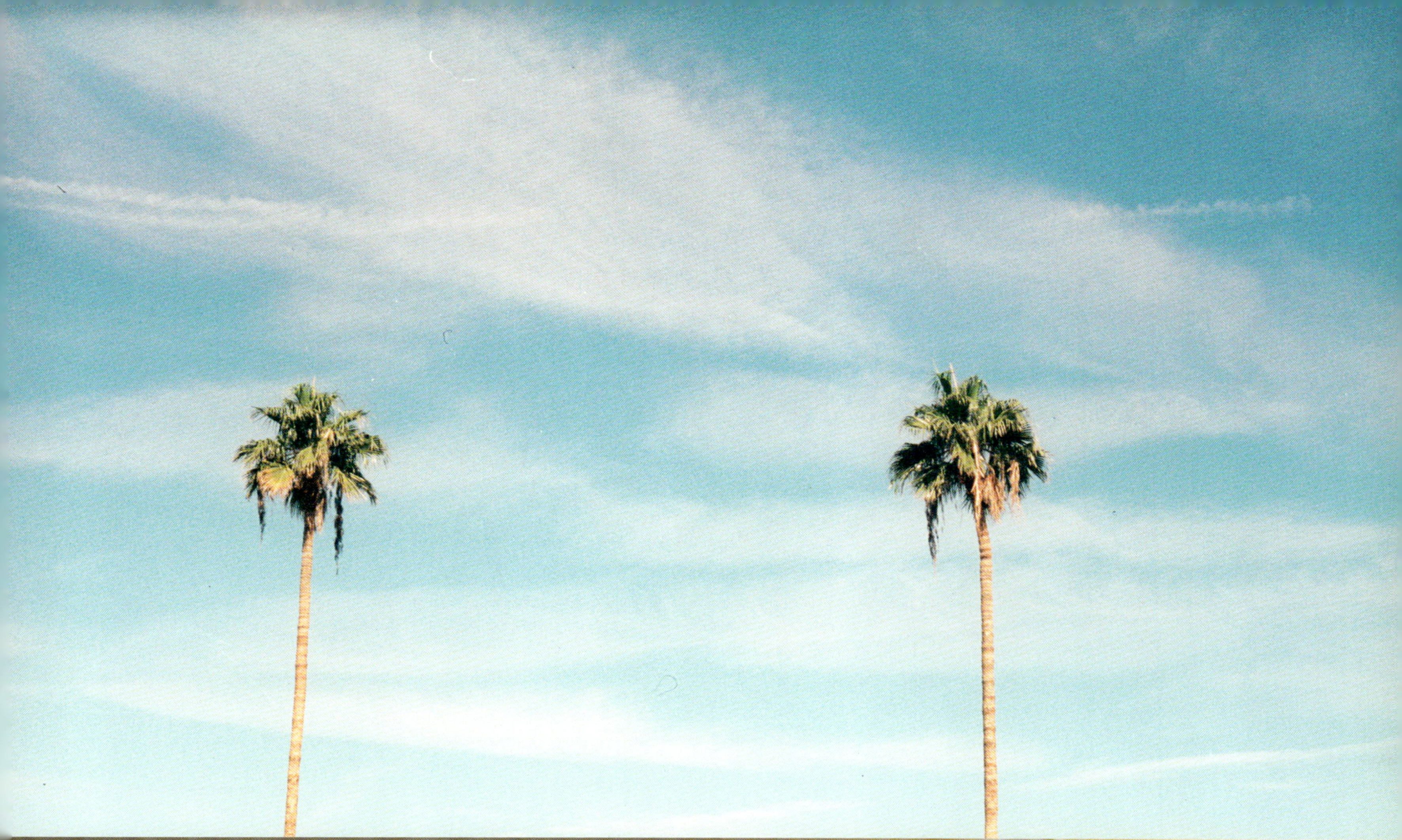

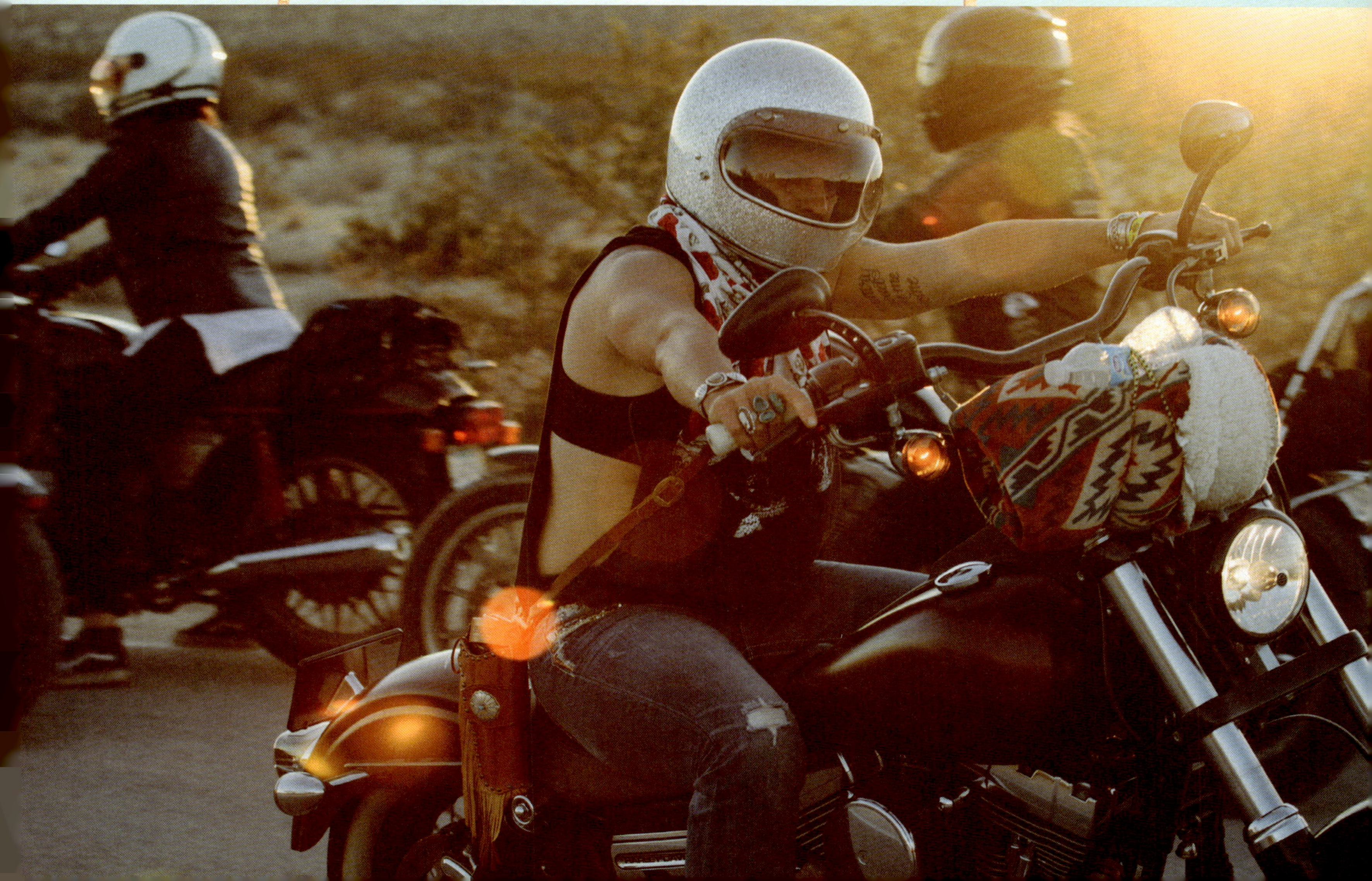

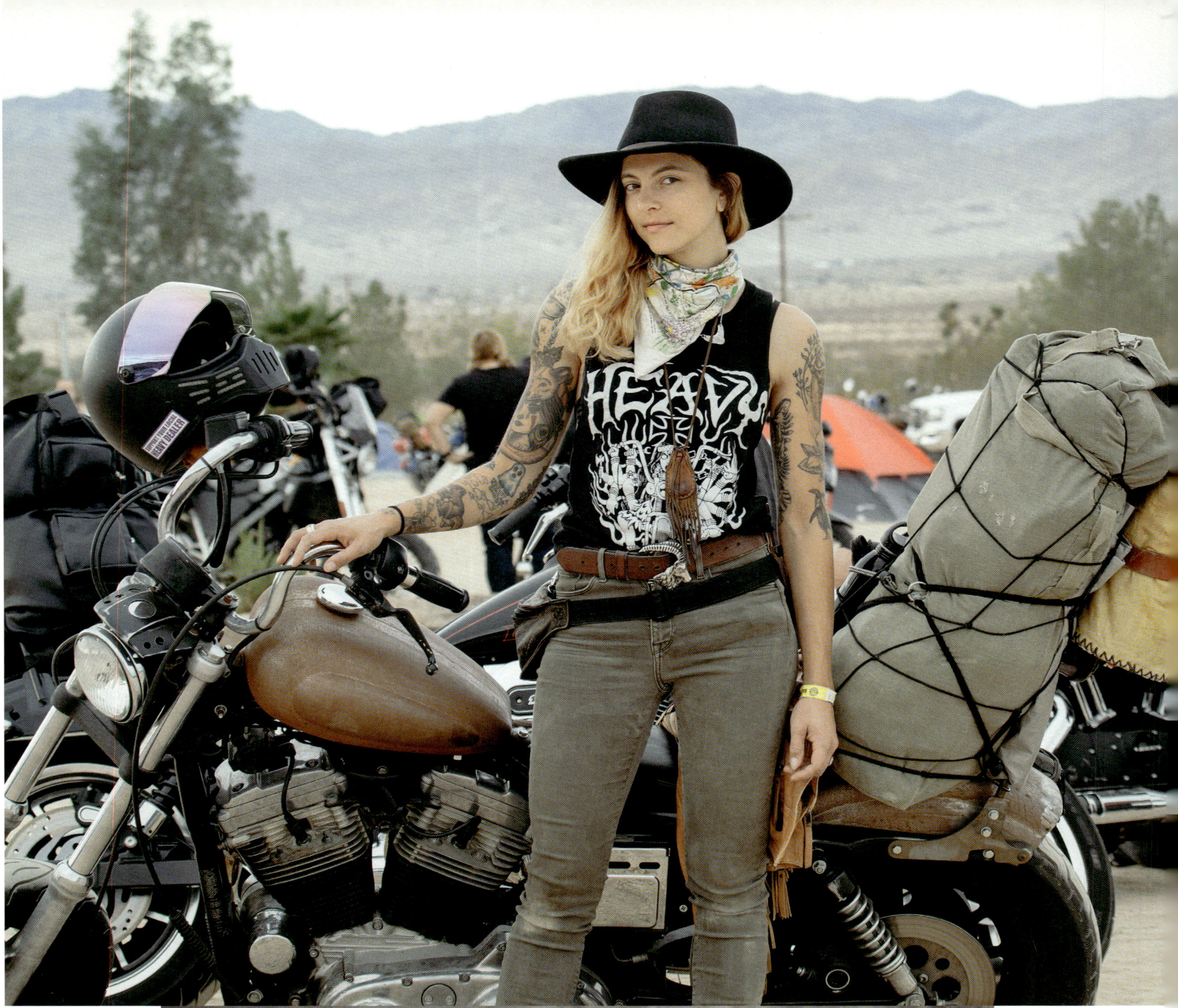

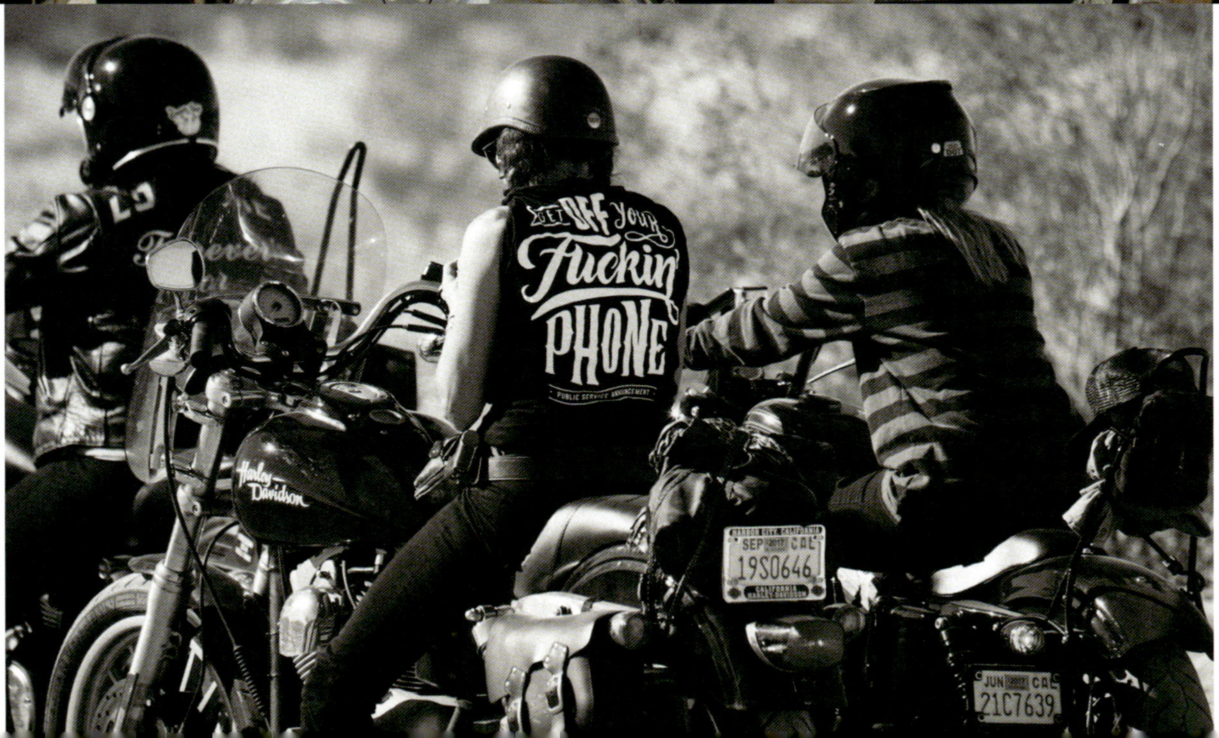
Fuckin
PHONE
19S0646
21C7639

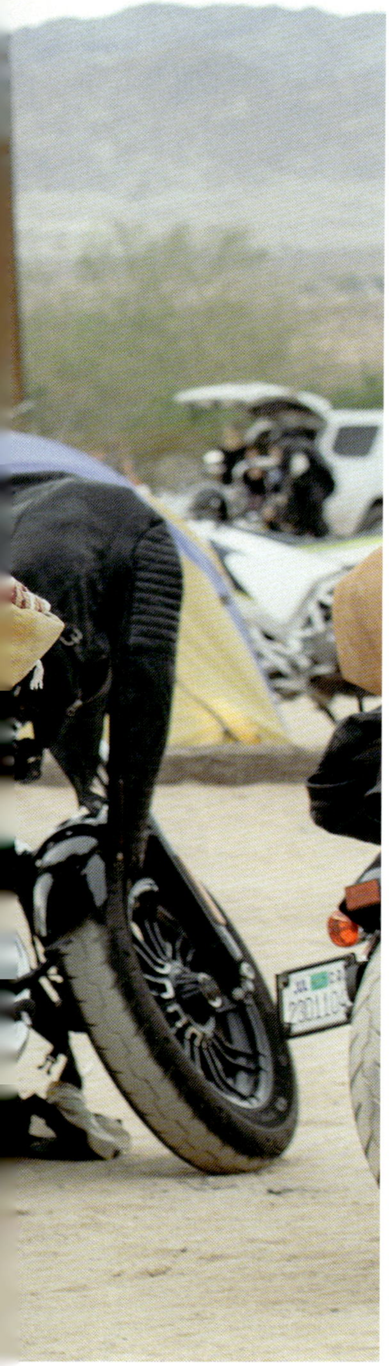

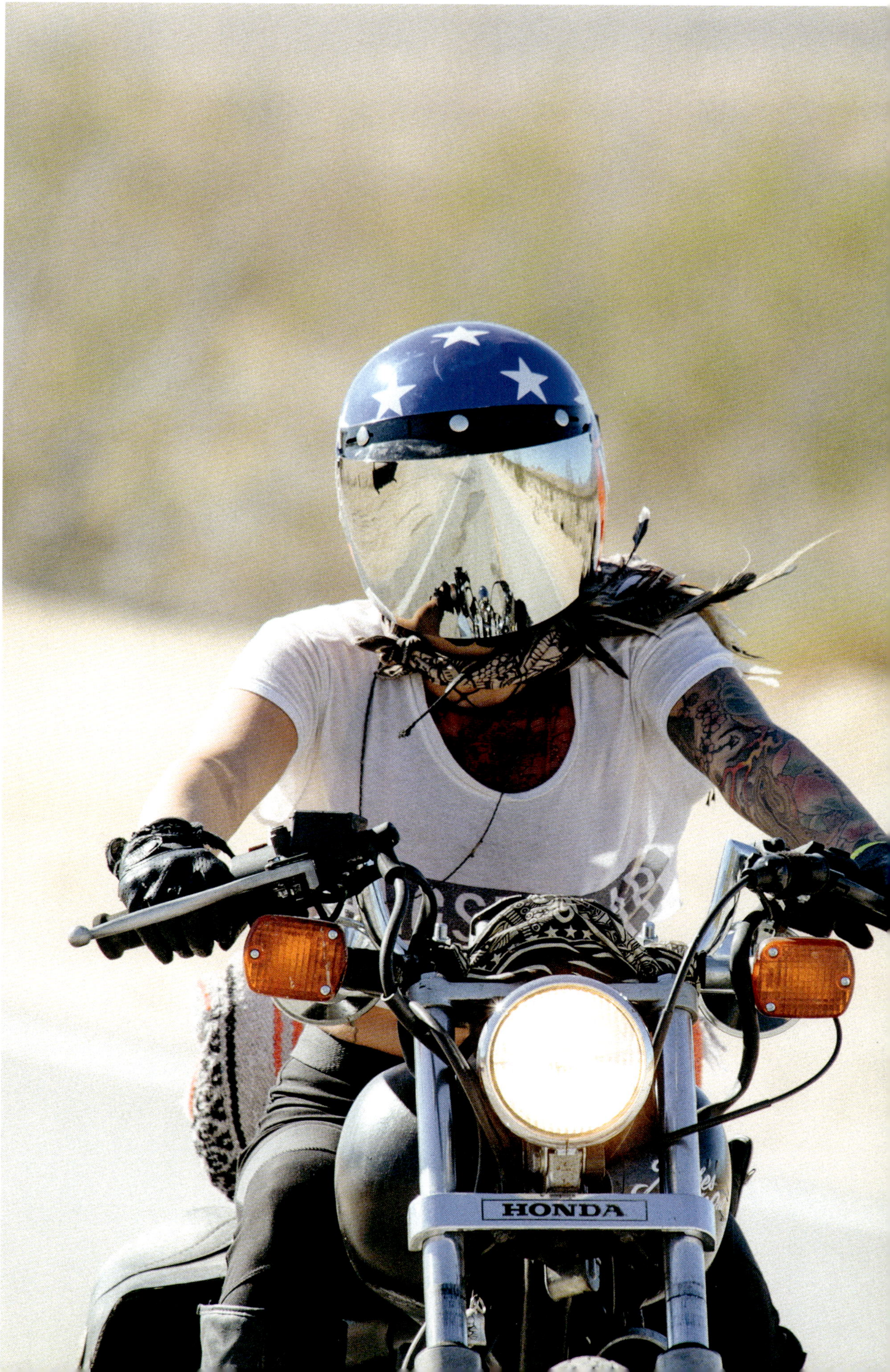
HONDA

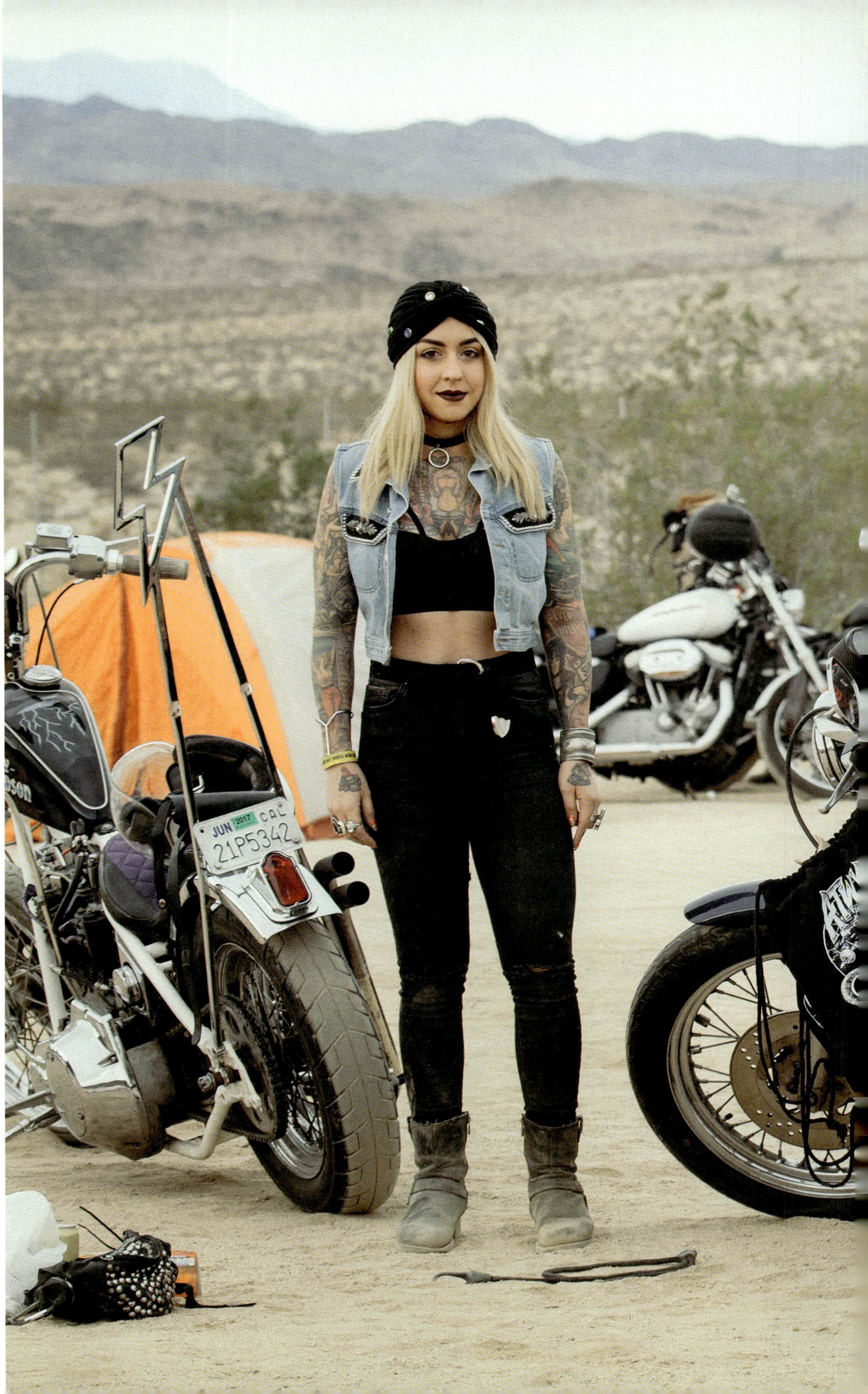
JUN 2017 CAL
21P5342

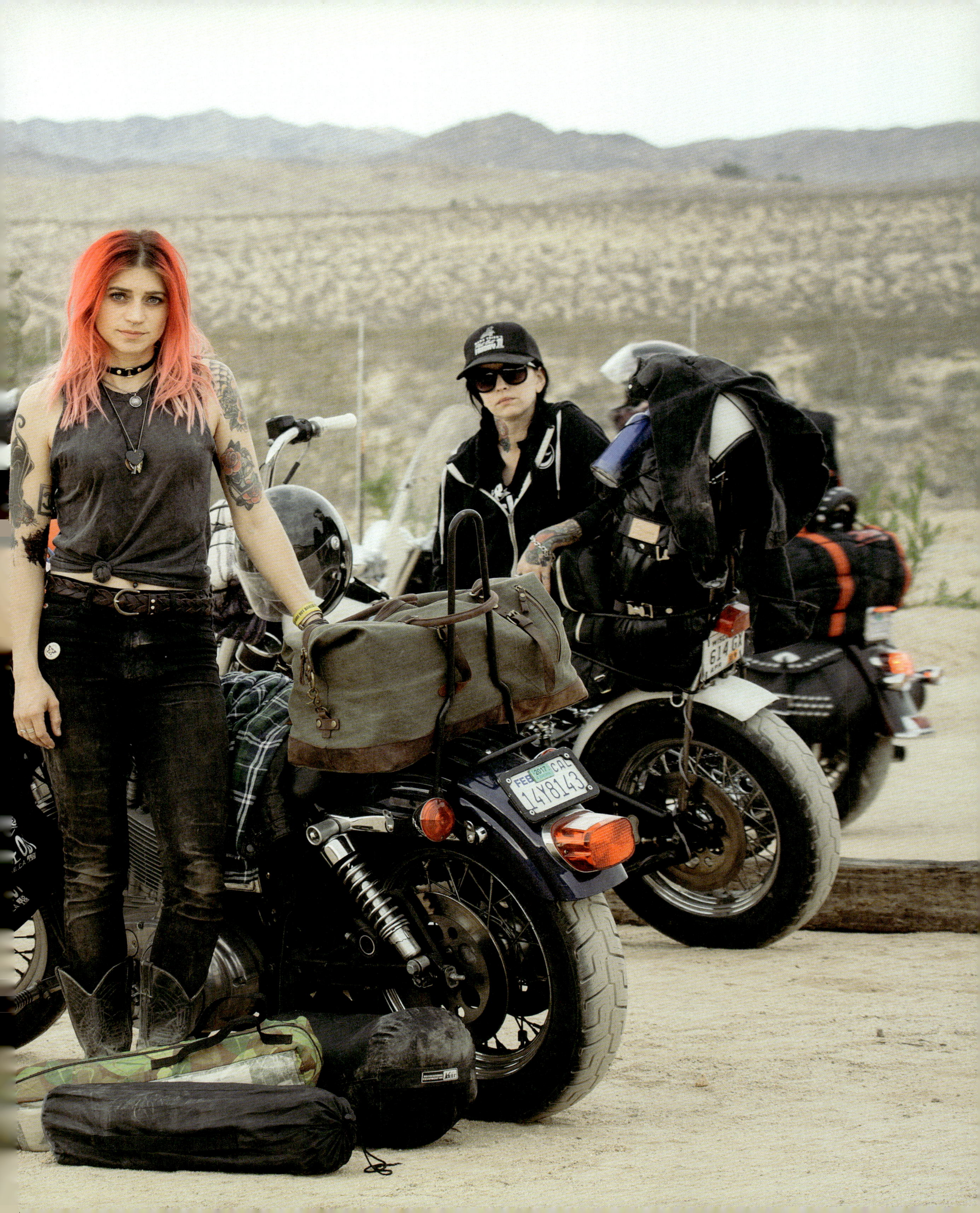
FEB 2017 CAL
14Y8143

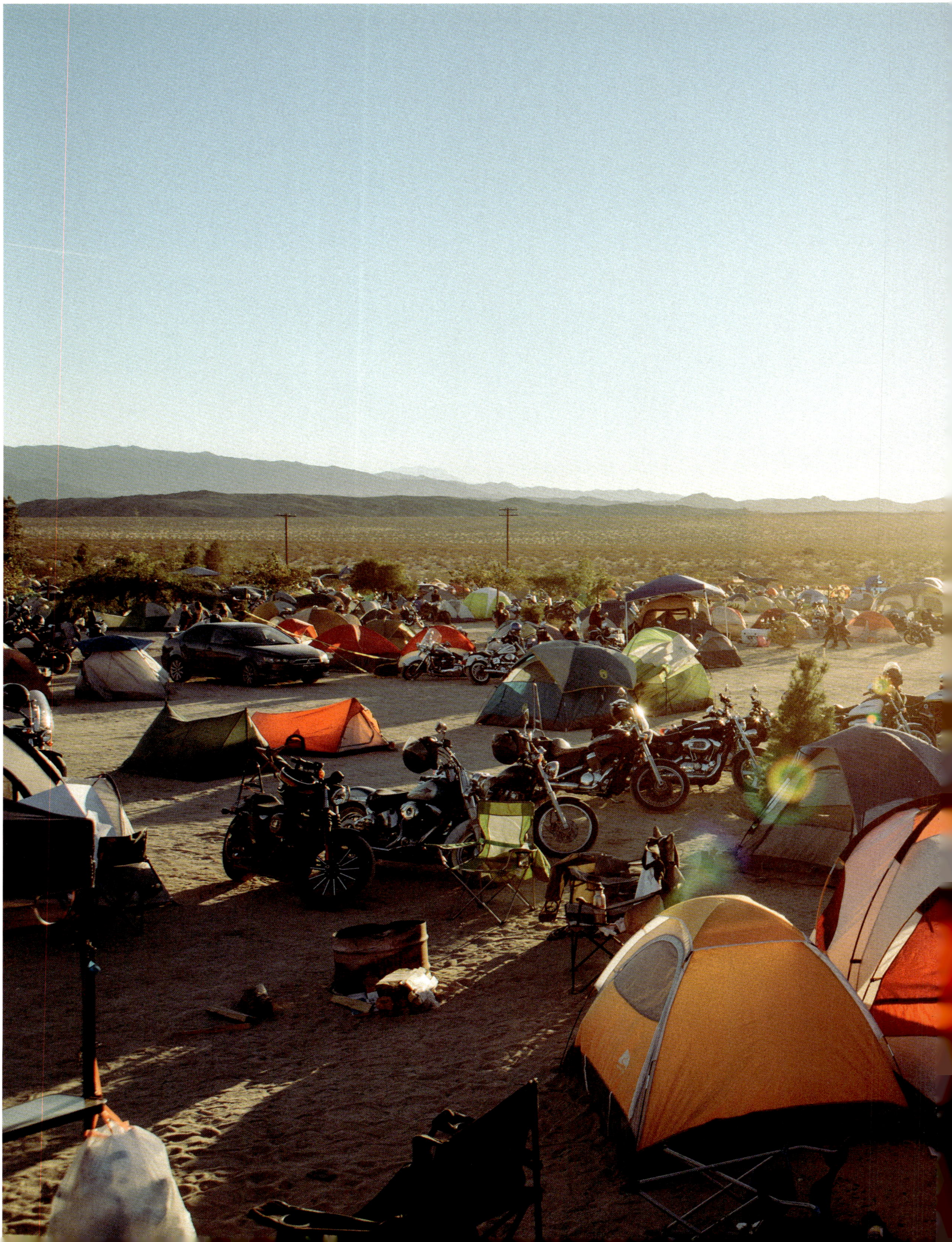

Joshua Tree/CA

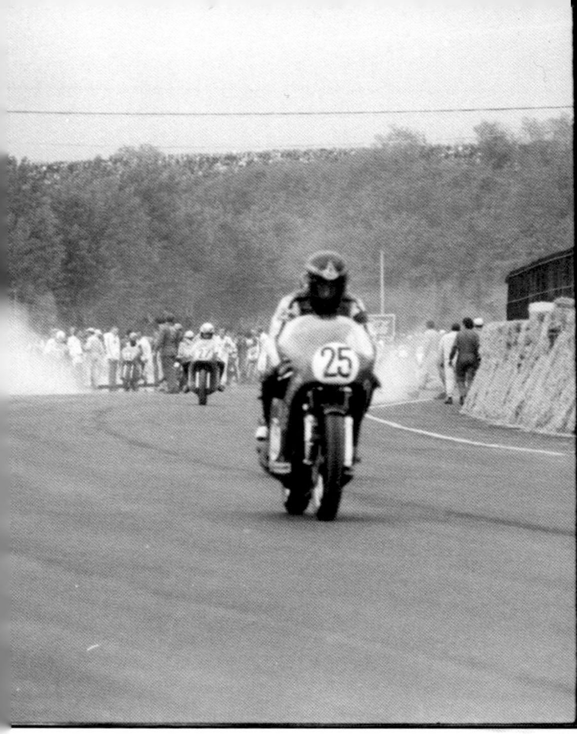

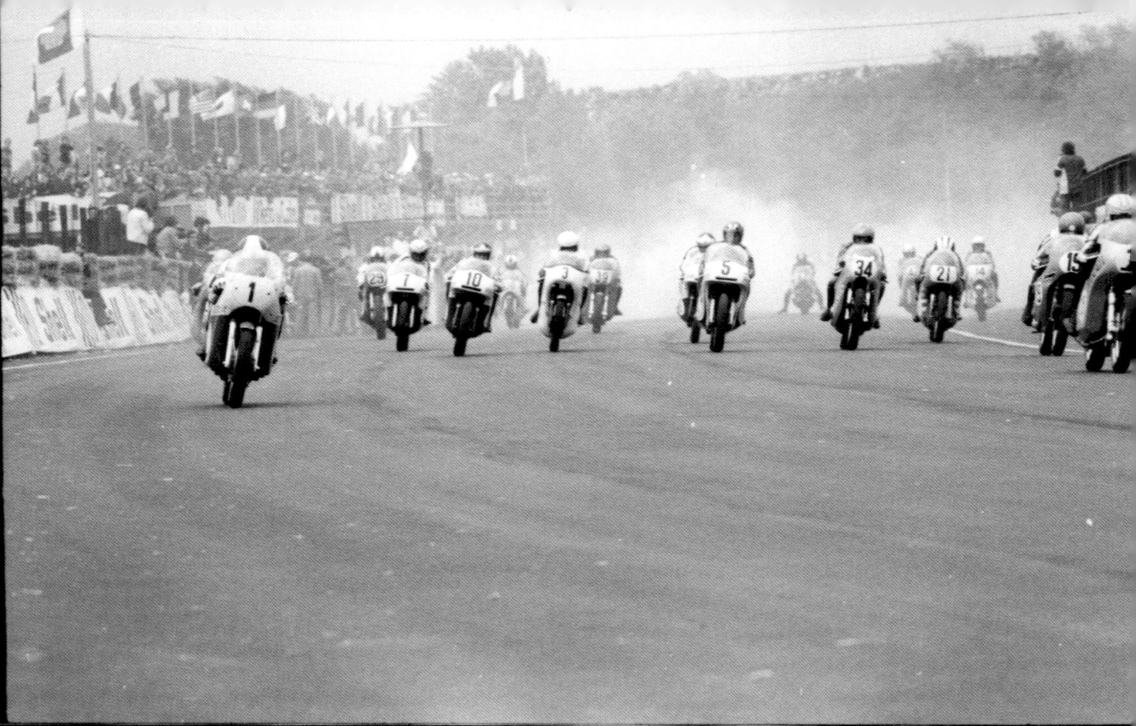
Shell

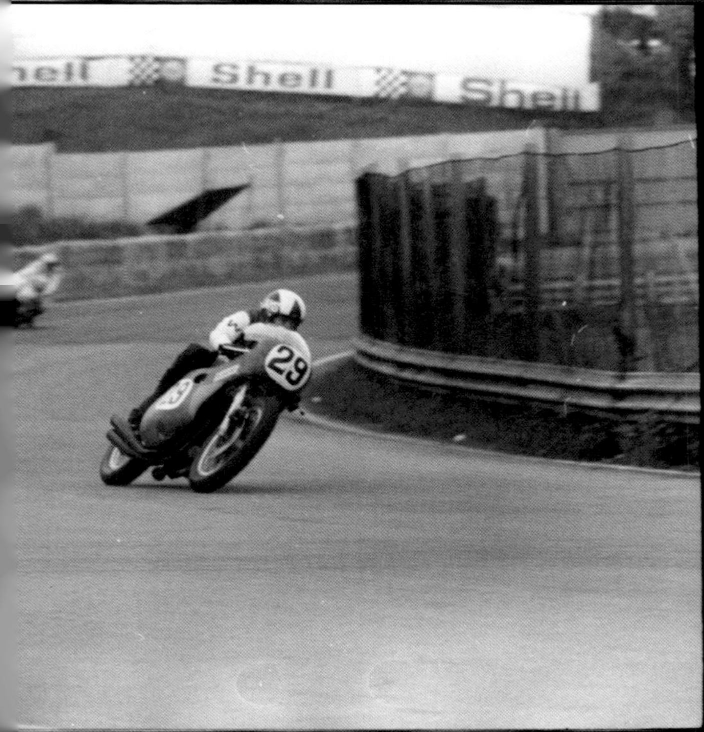
Shell
Shell

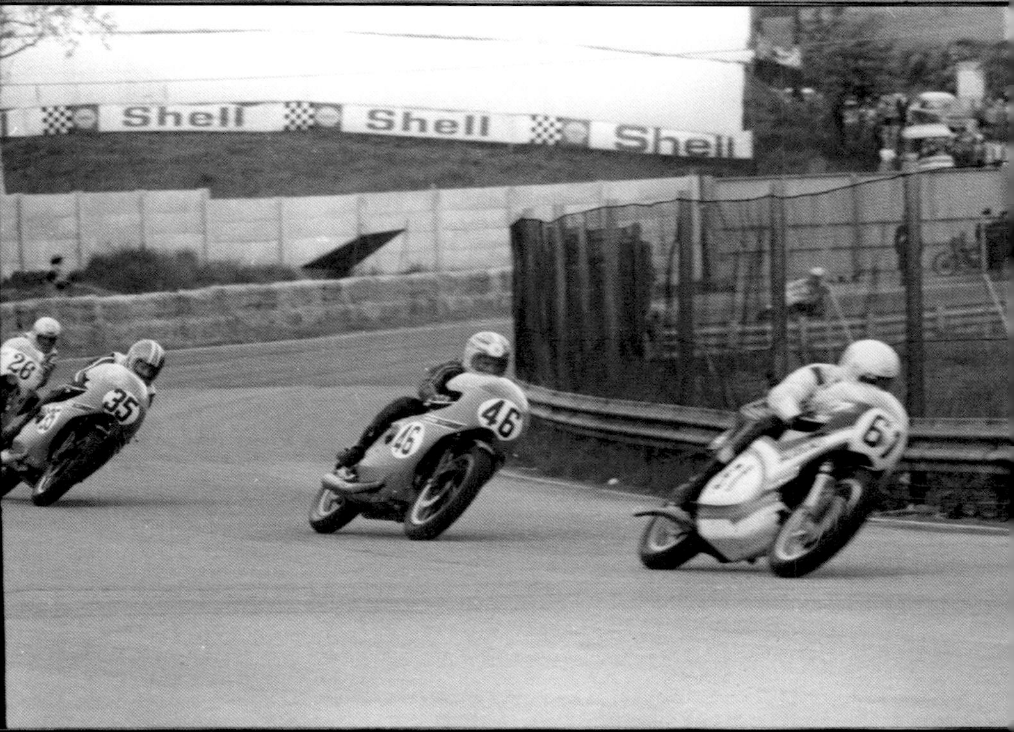
Shell
Shell
Shell

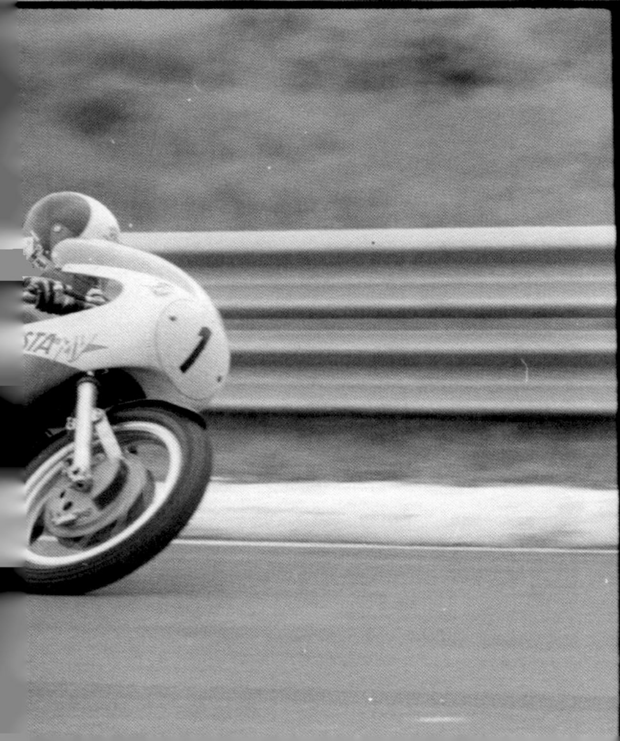

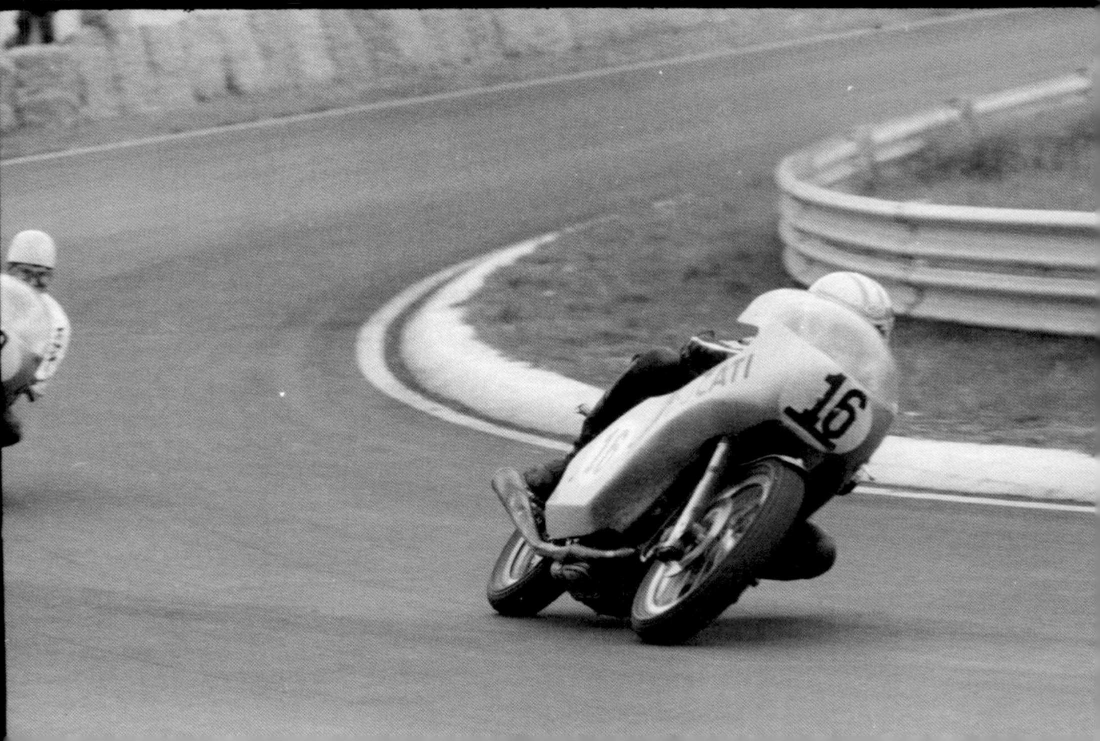

Shell
Shell
Shell

DUCATI
16
16

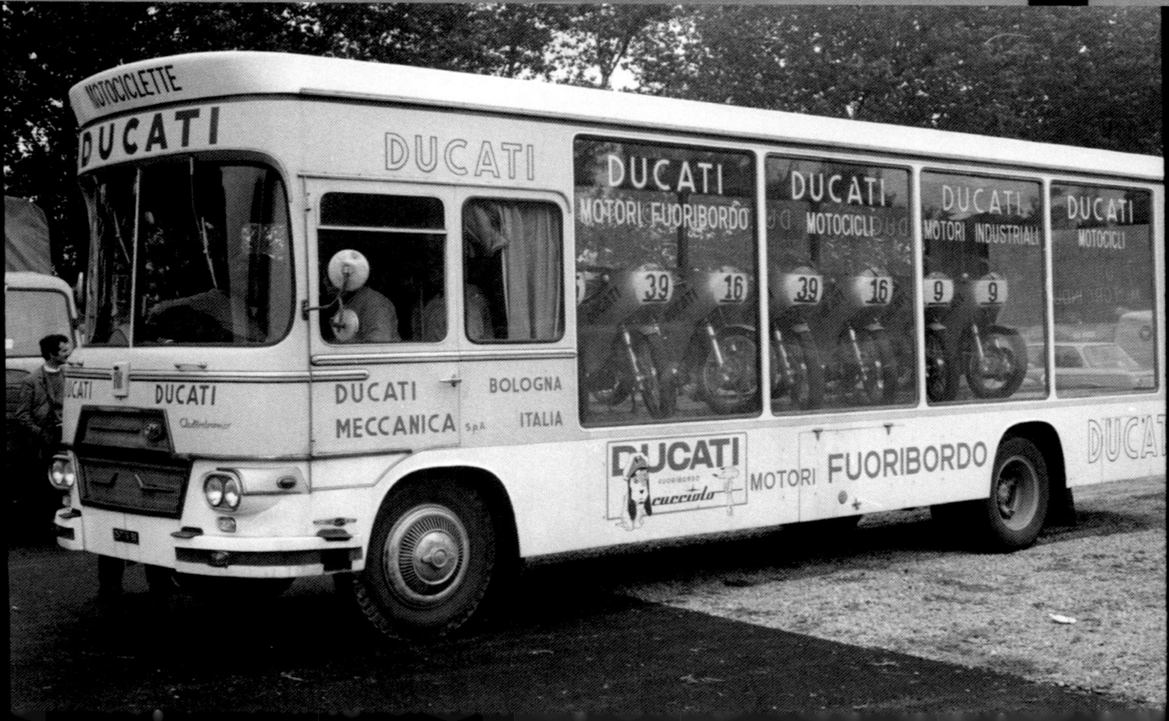
MOTOCICLETTE
DUCATI
DUCATI
DUCATI
MOTORI FUORIBORDO
DUCATI
MOTOCICLI
DUCATI
MOTORI INDUSTRIALI
DUCATI
MOTOCICLI
DUCATI
DUCATI
DUCATI
MECCANICA
S.p.A.
BOLOGNA
ITALIA
DUCATI
MOTORI
FUORIBORDO
DUCATI

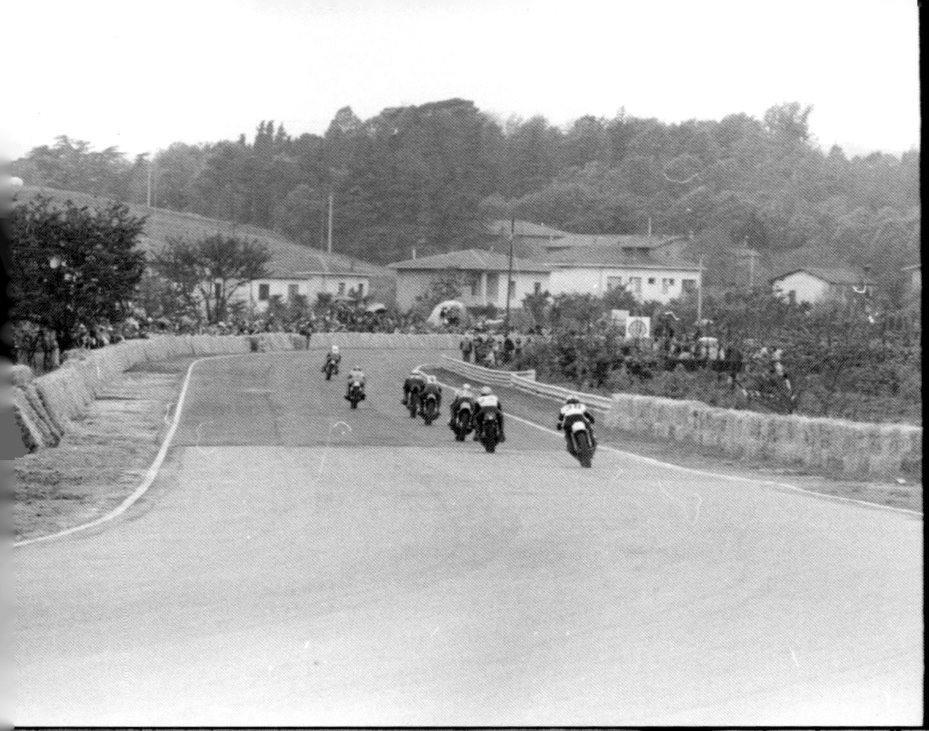
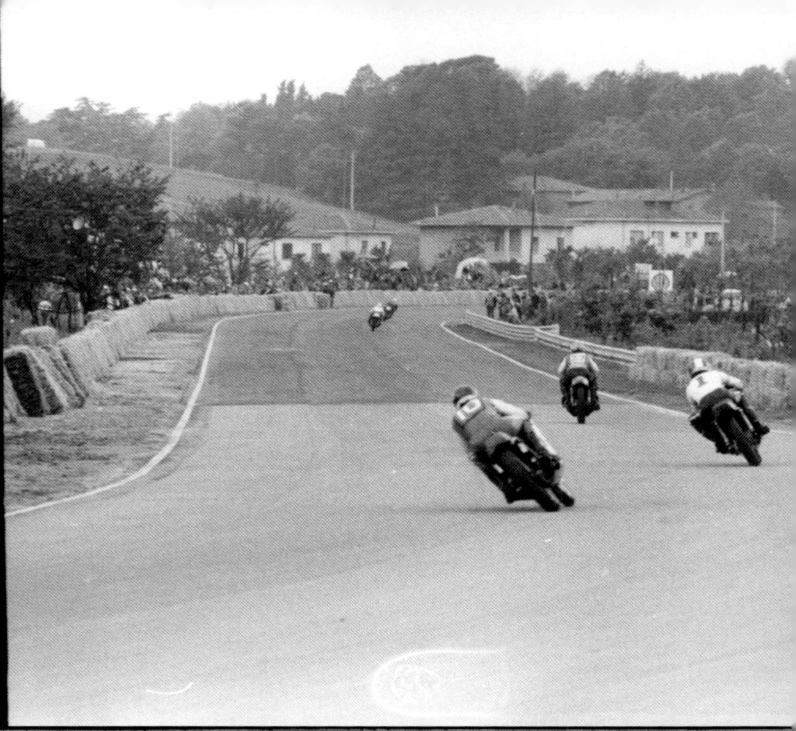
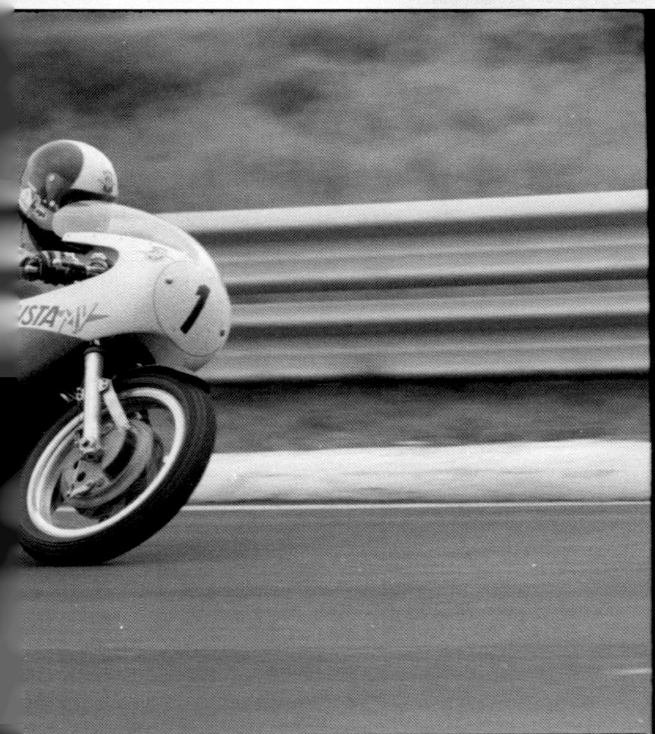
1
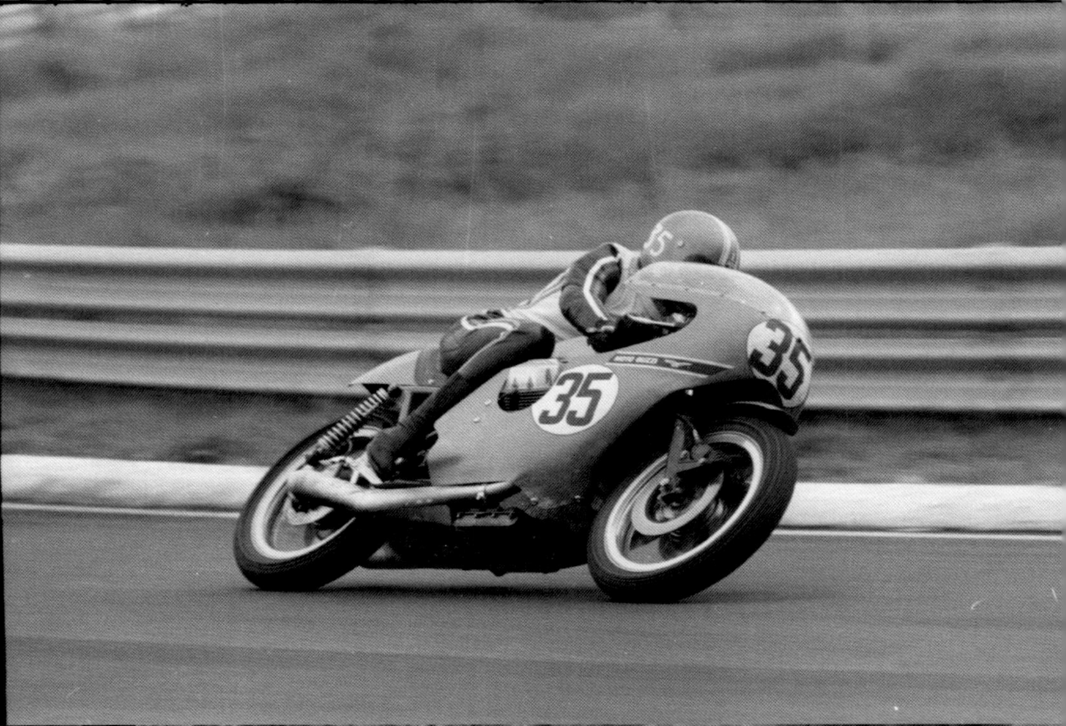
35
35
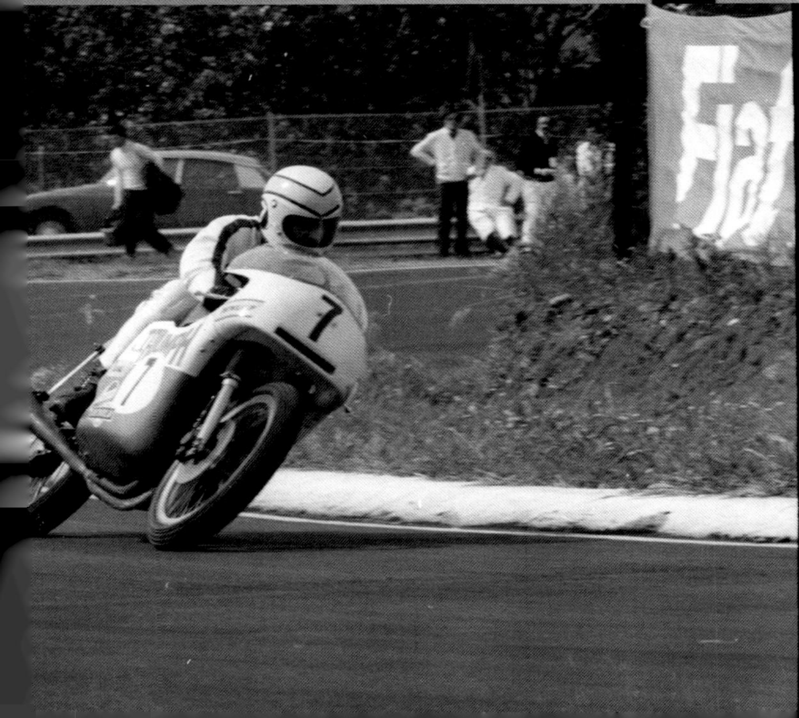
7
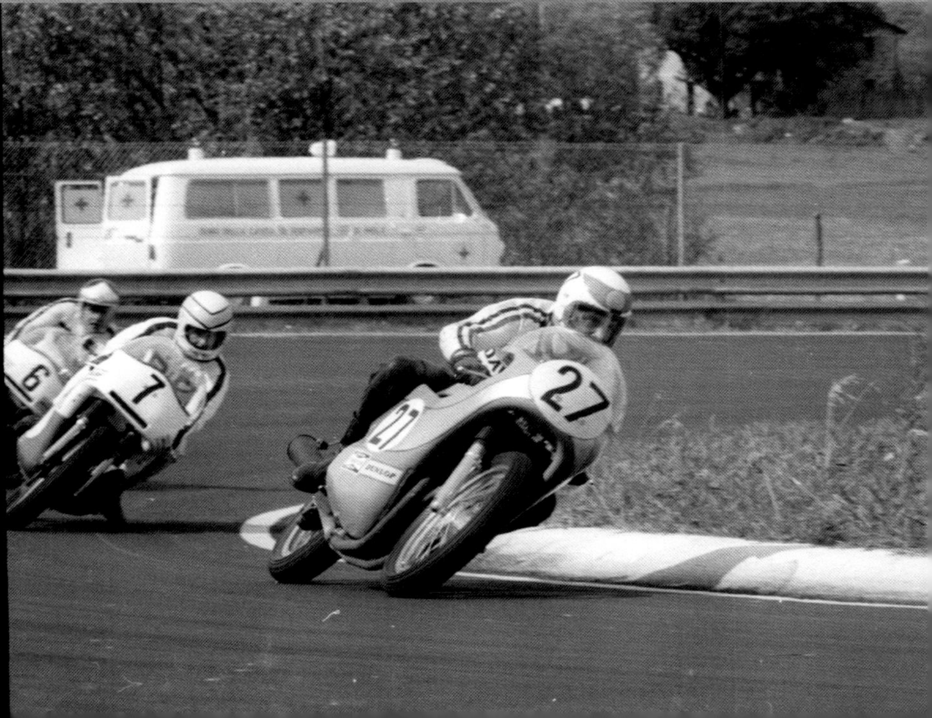
6
7
27

SPAGGIARI
9

19
16

61
SUZUKI
DUNLOP

47
rga
ITALCAVA

DUCATI
9

AGUSTA
1

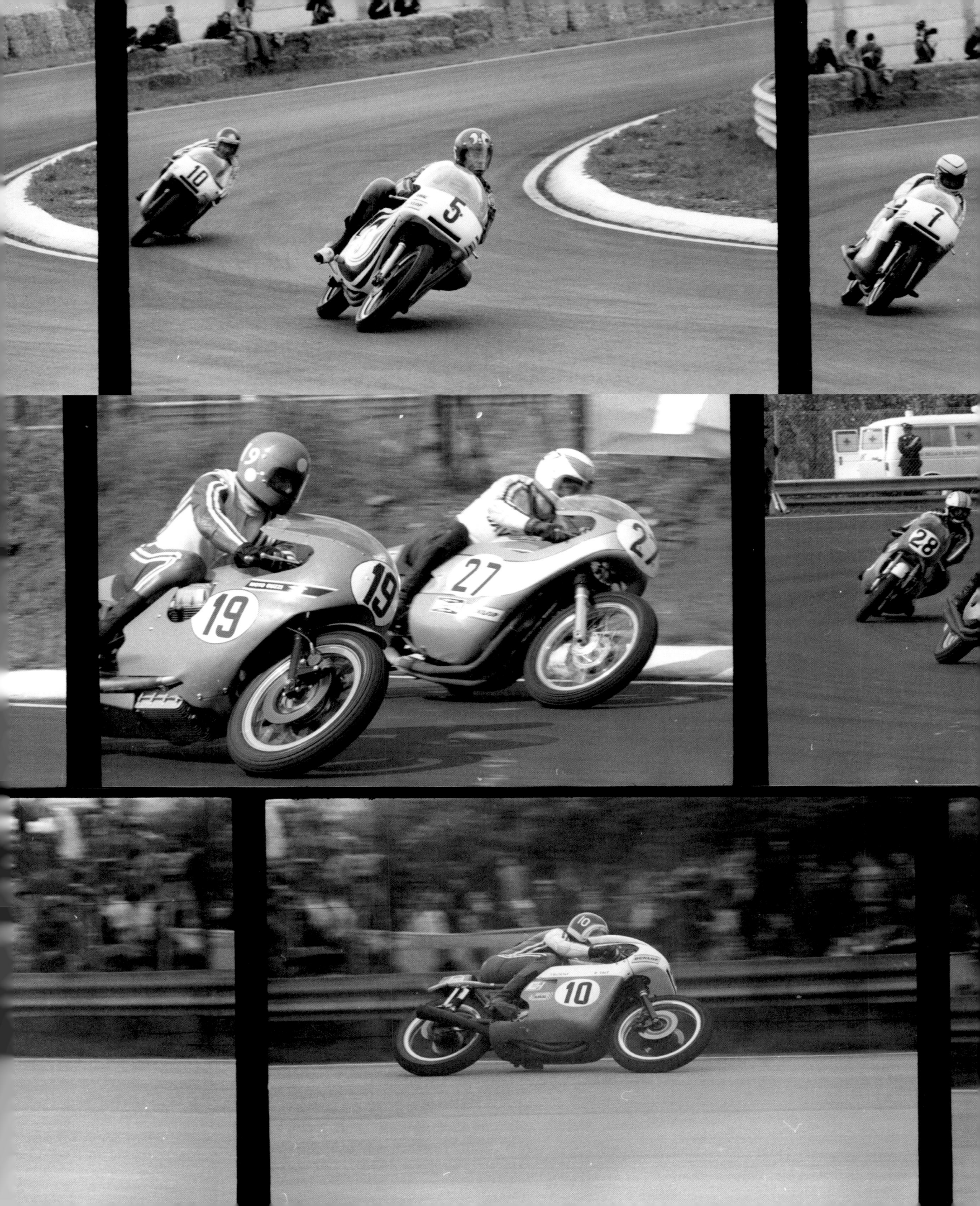
10
5
7
19
27
28
DUNLOP

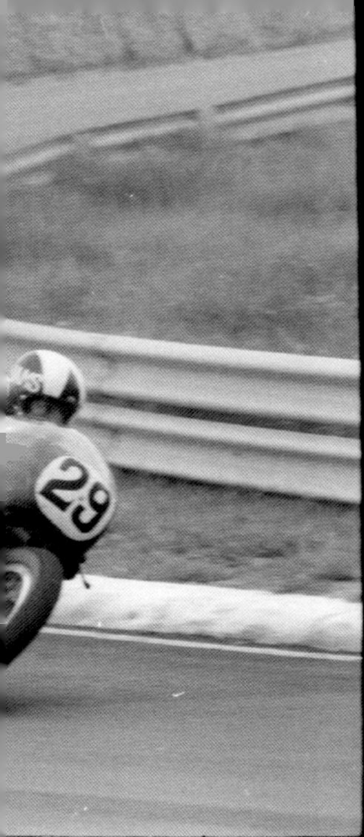

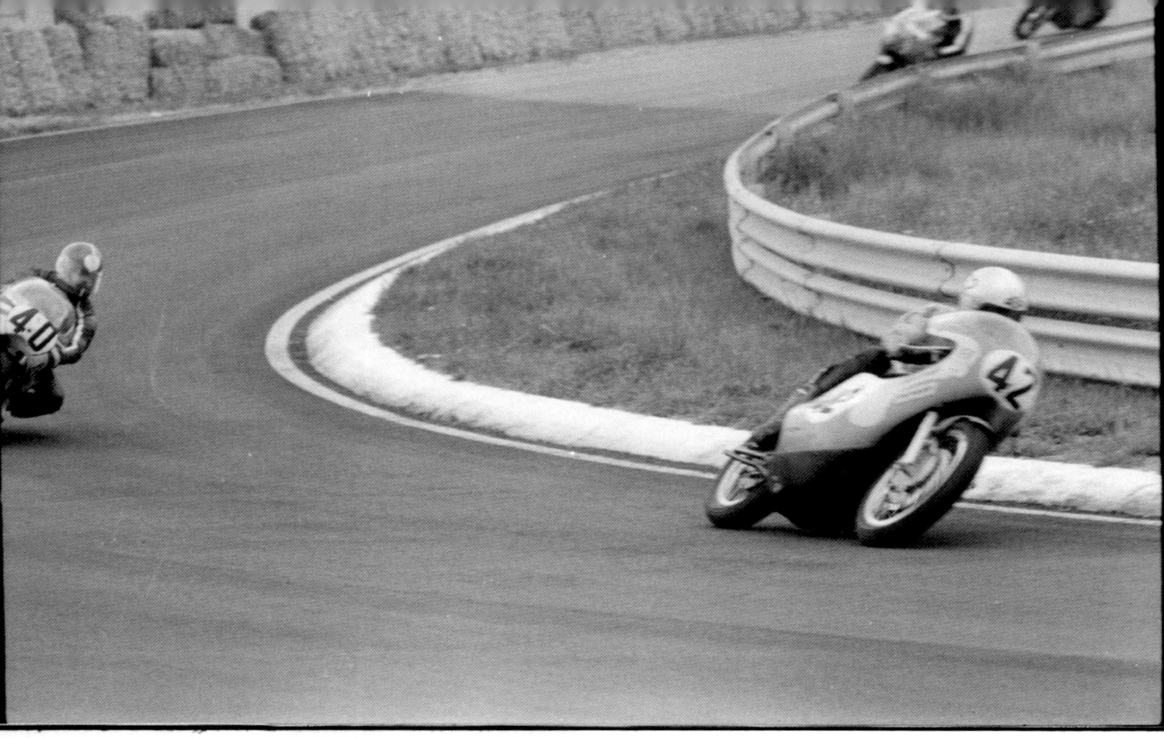

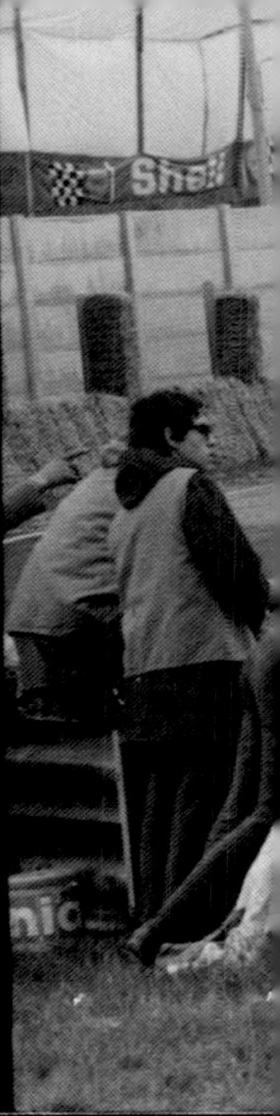
Shell

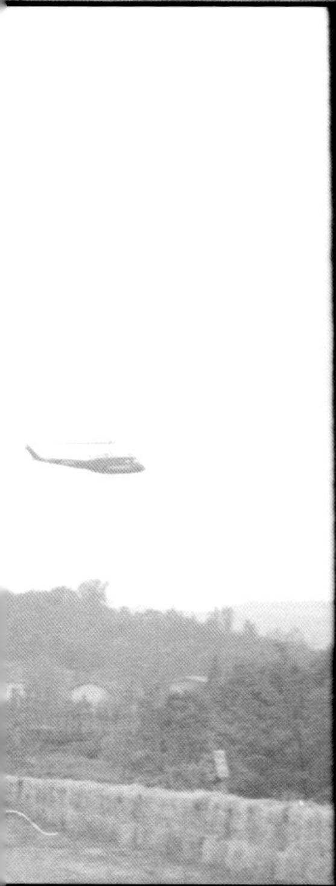

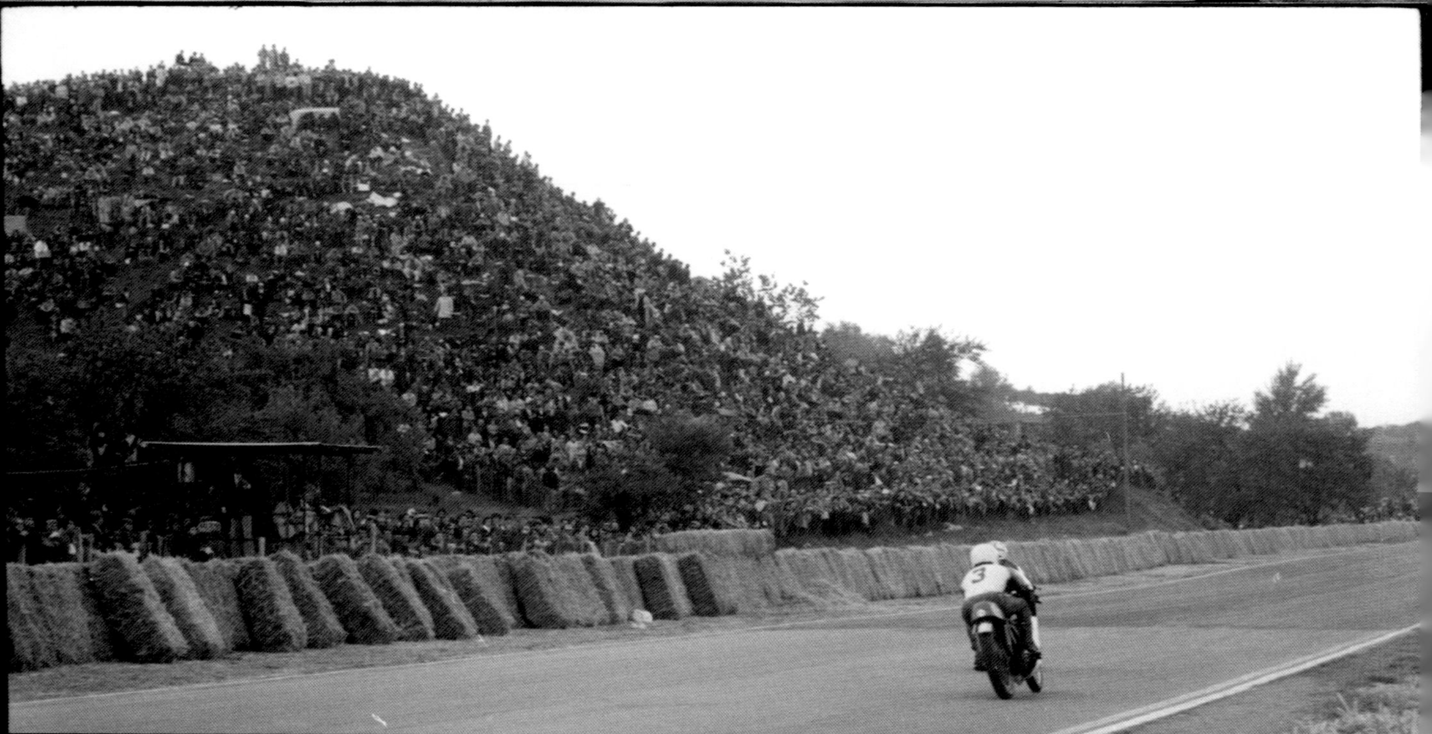

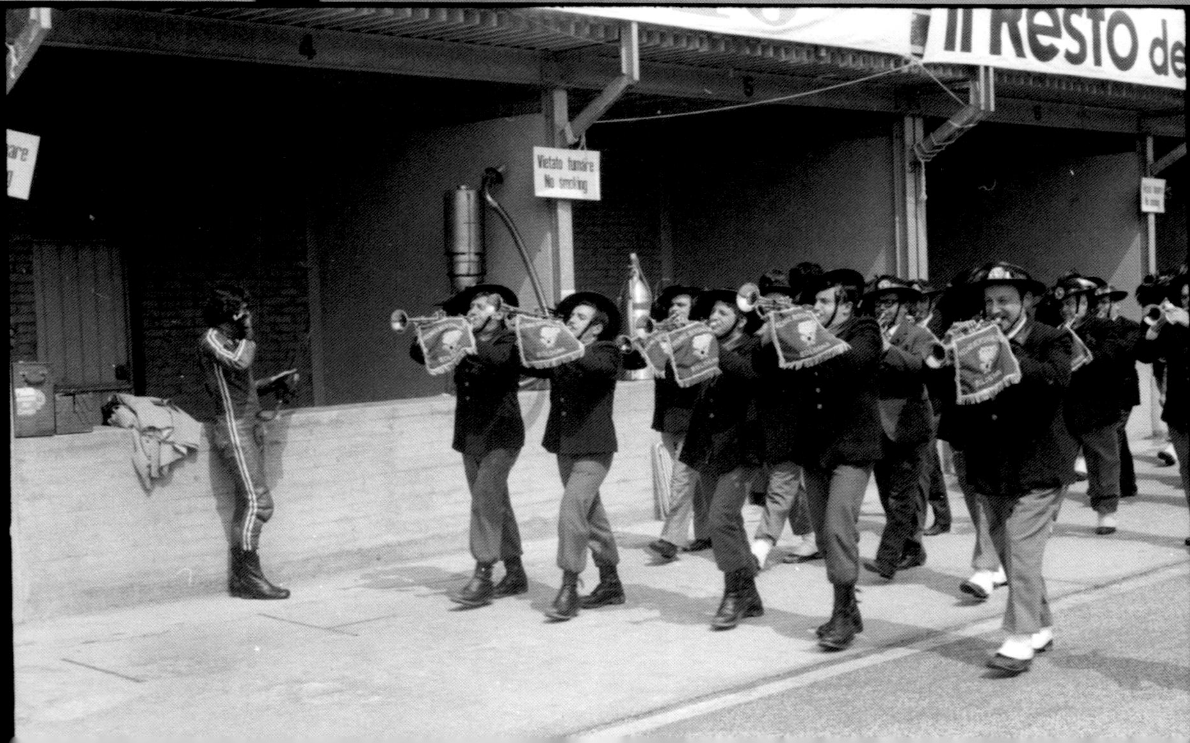
Il Resto de
Vietato fumare
No smoking

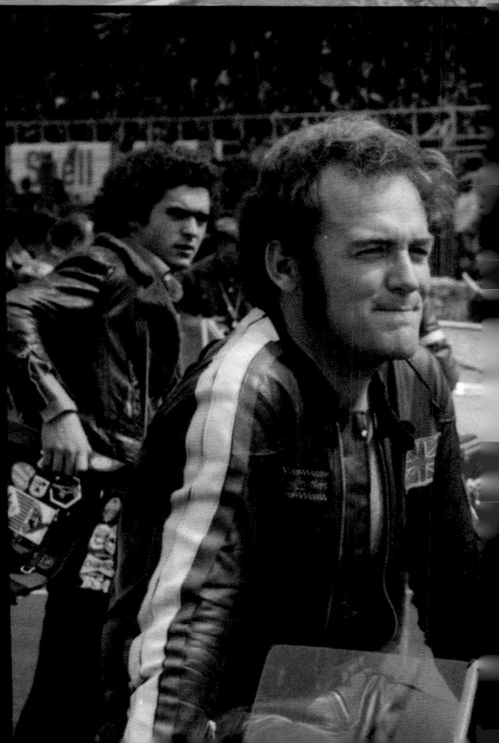
Shell

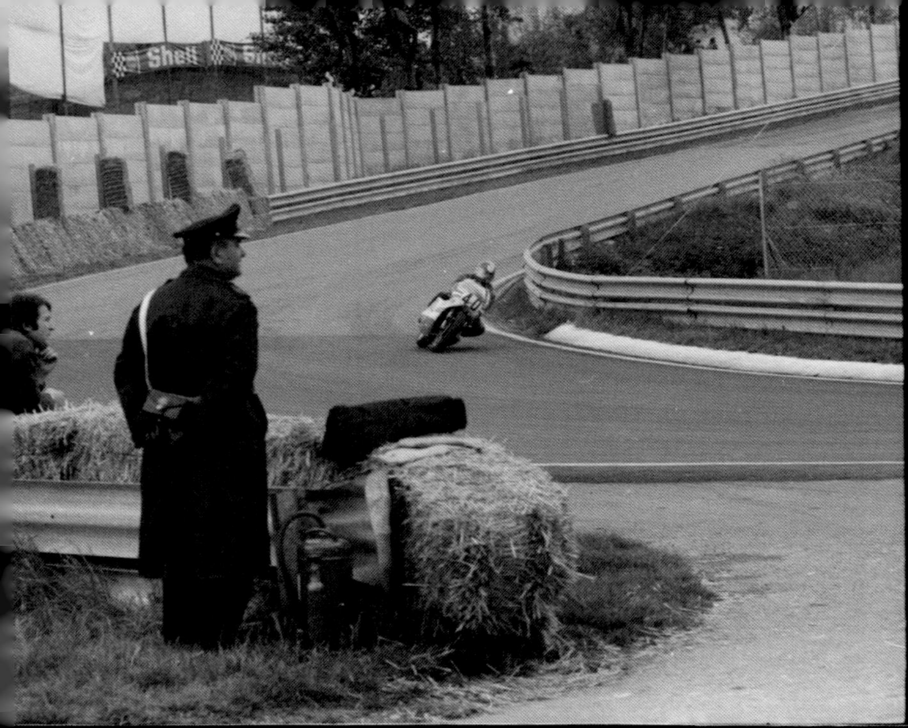
Shell

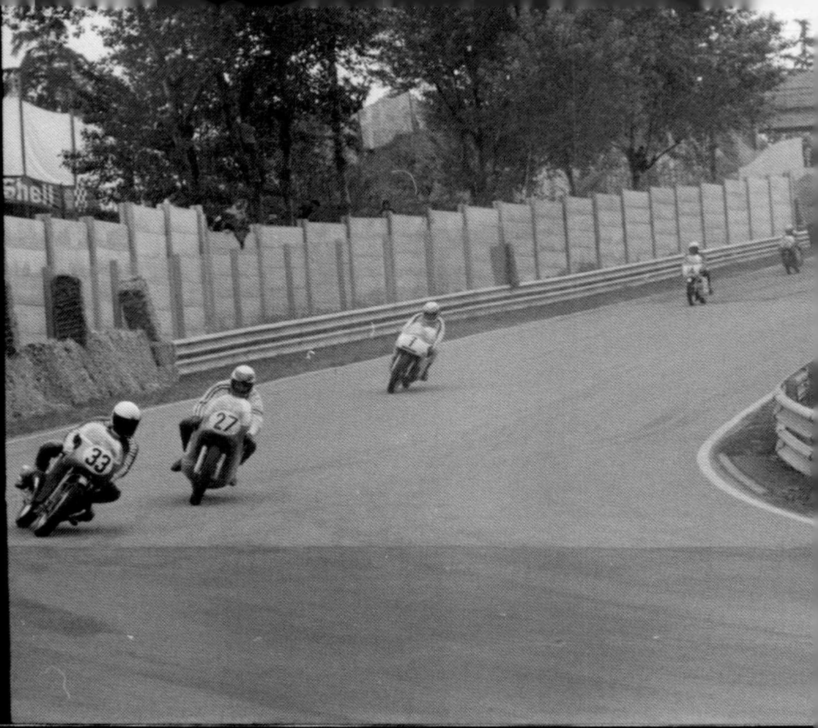
Shell
33
27

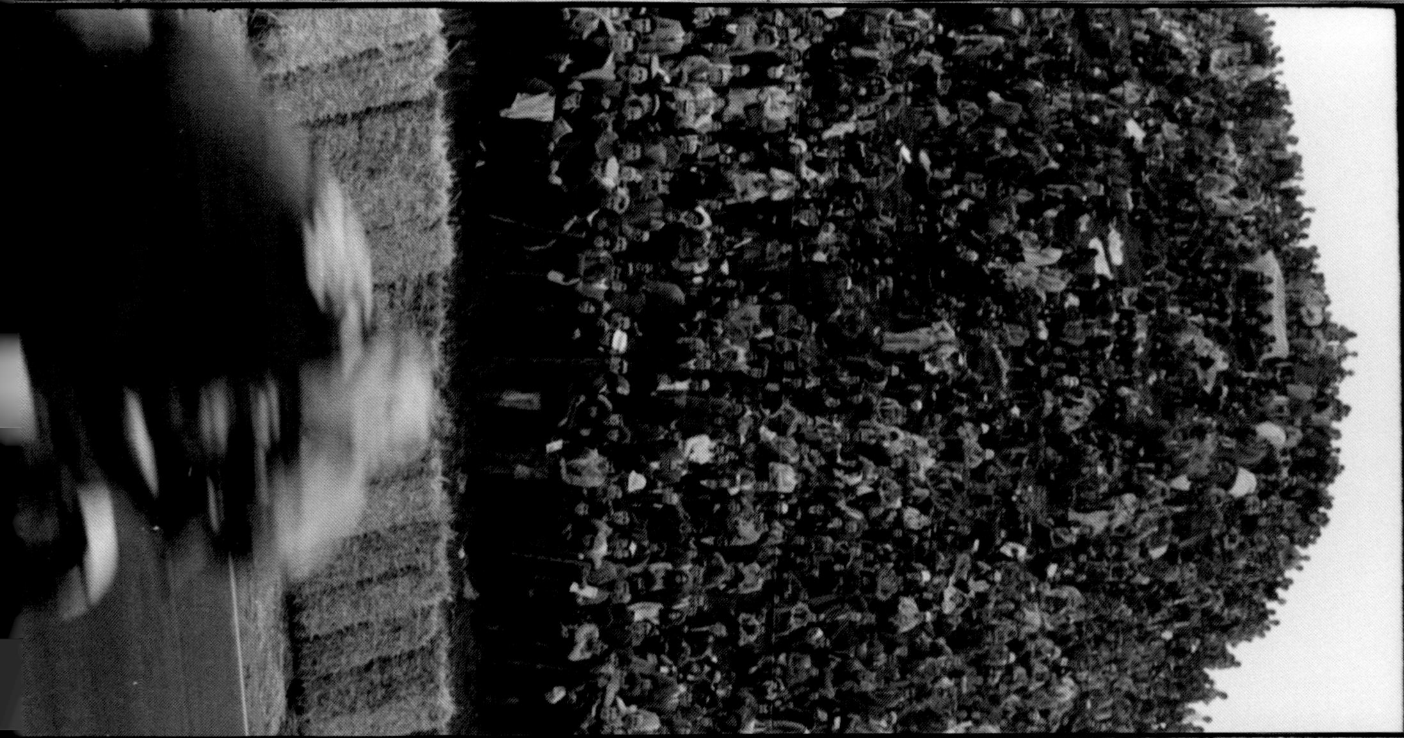

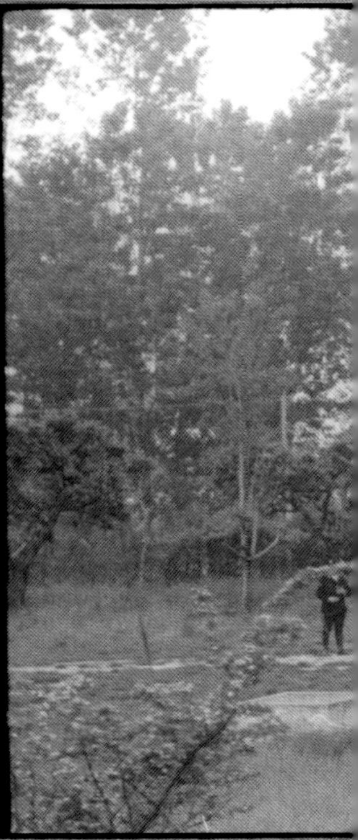

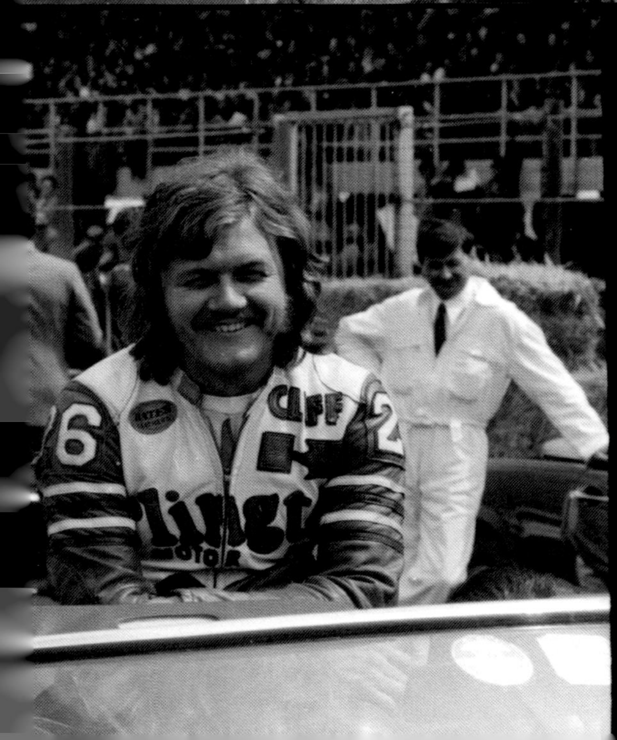
CLIFF

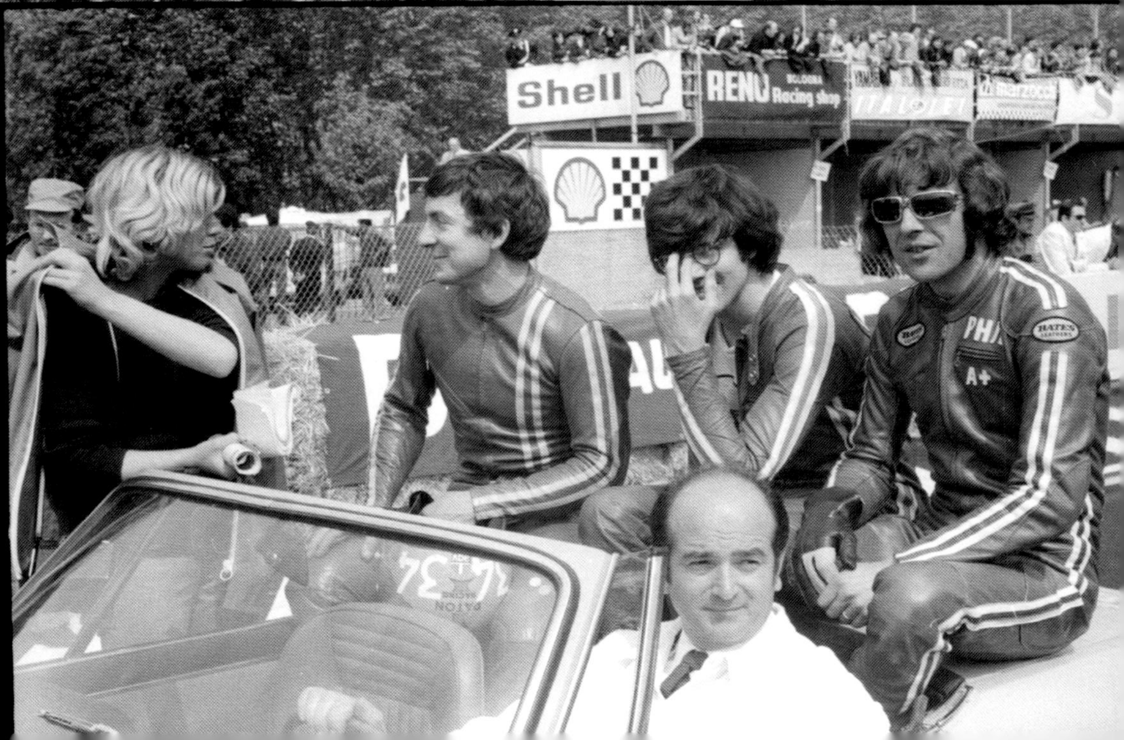
Shell
Racing shop

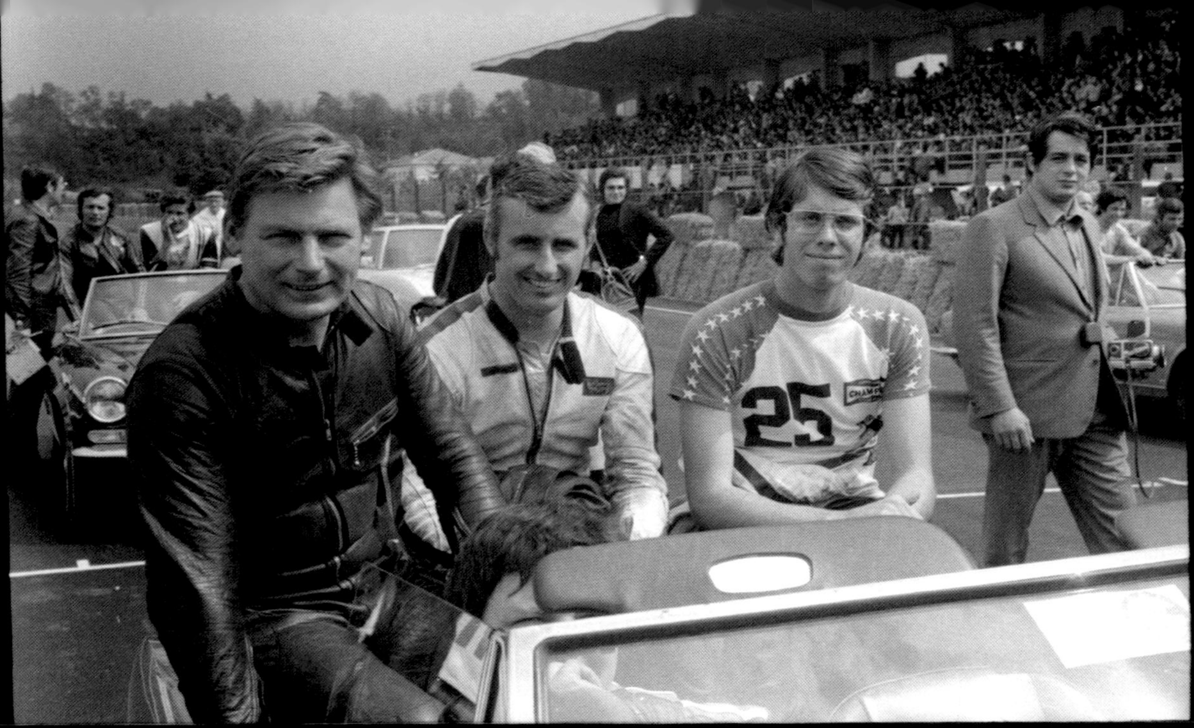
25

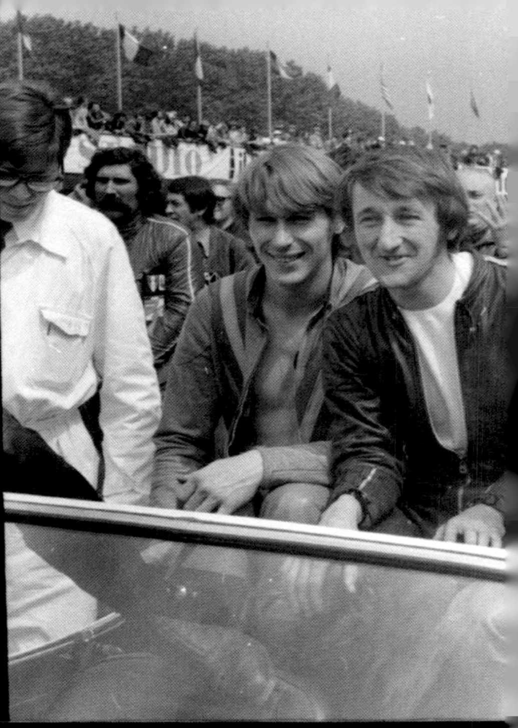

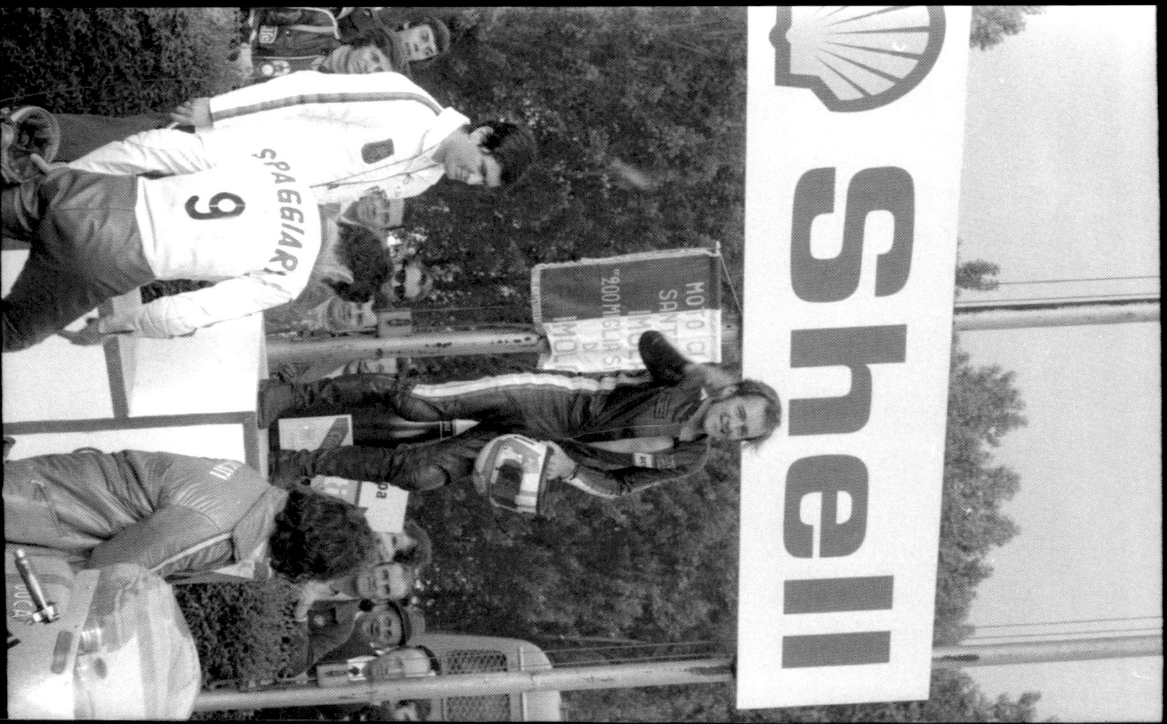
SPAGGIARI
9
Shell

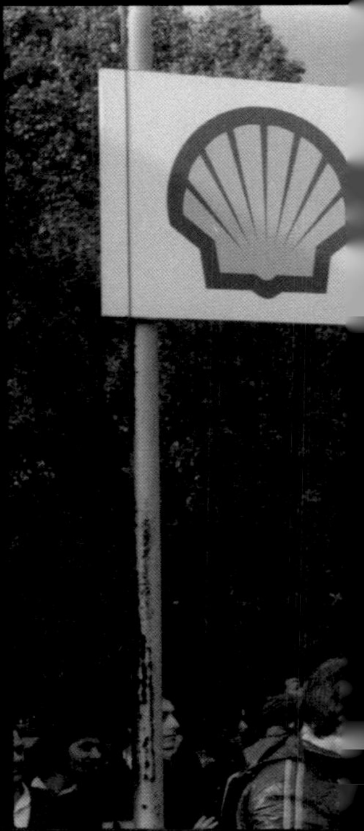

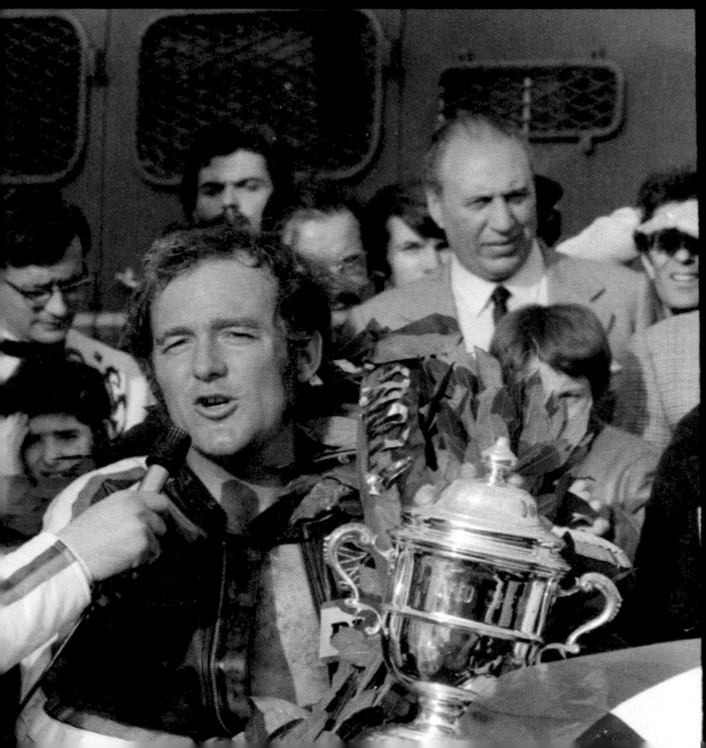

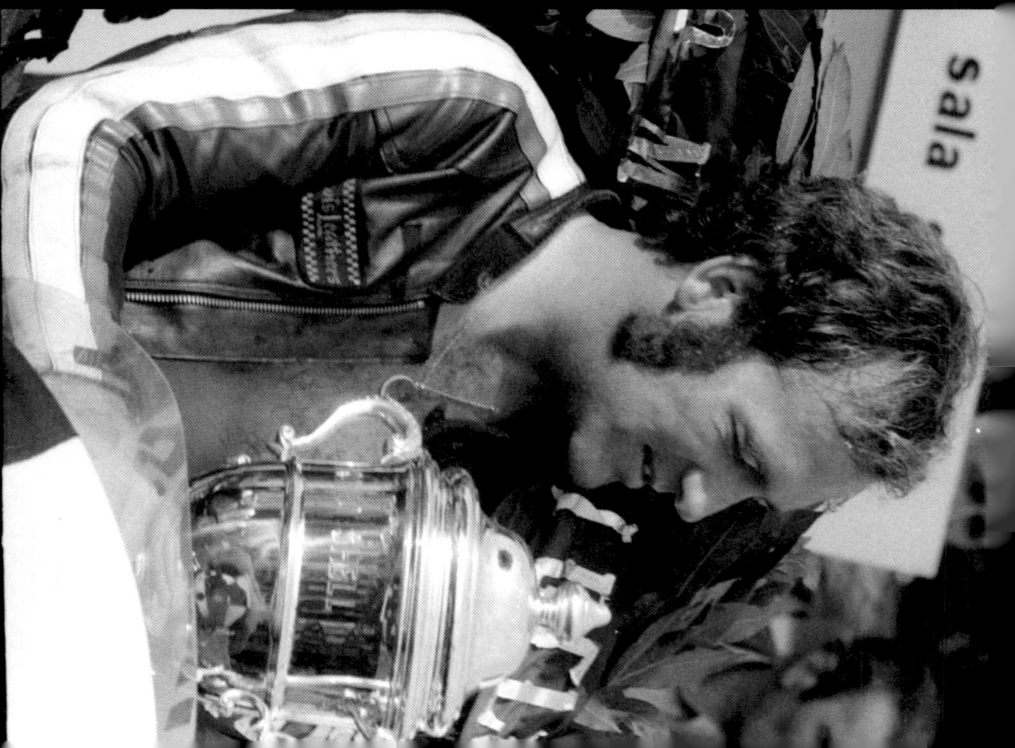
sala

Shell
Shell
FIAT

Shell
MOTO CLUB
SANTERNO
IMOLA
200 MIGLIA SHELL
DI
IMOLA

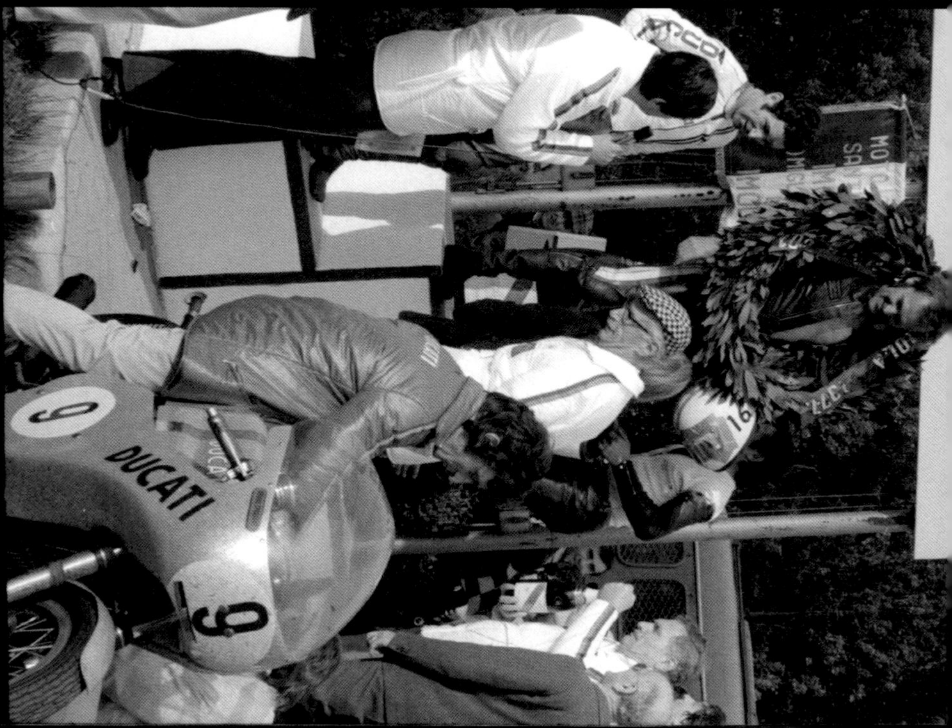
DUCATI

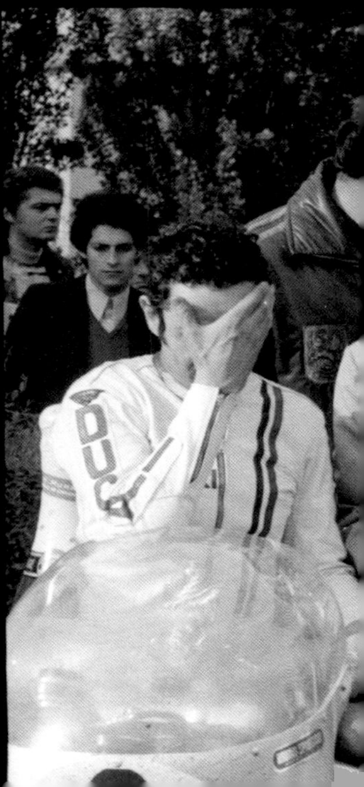

Focus
フォーカス

Dimitri Coste

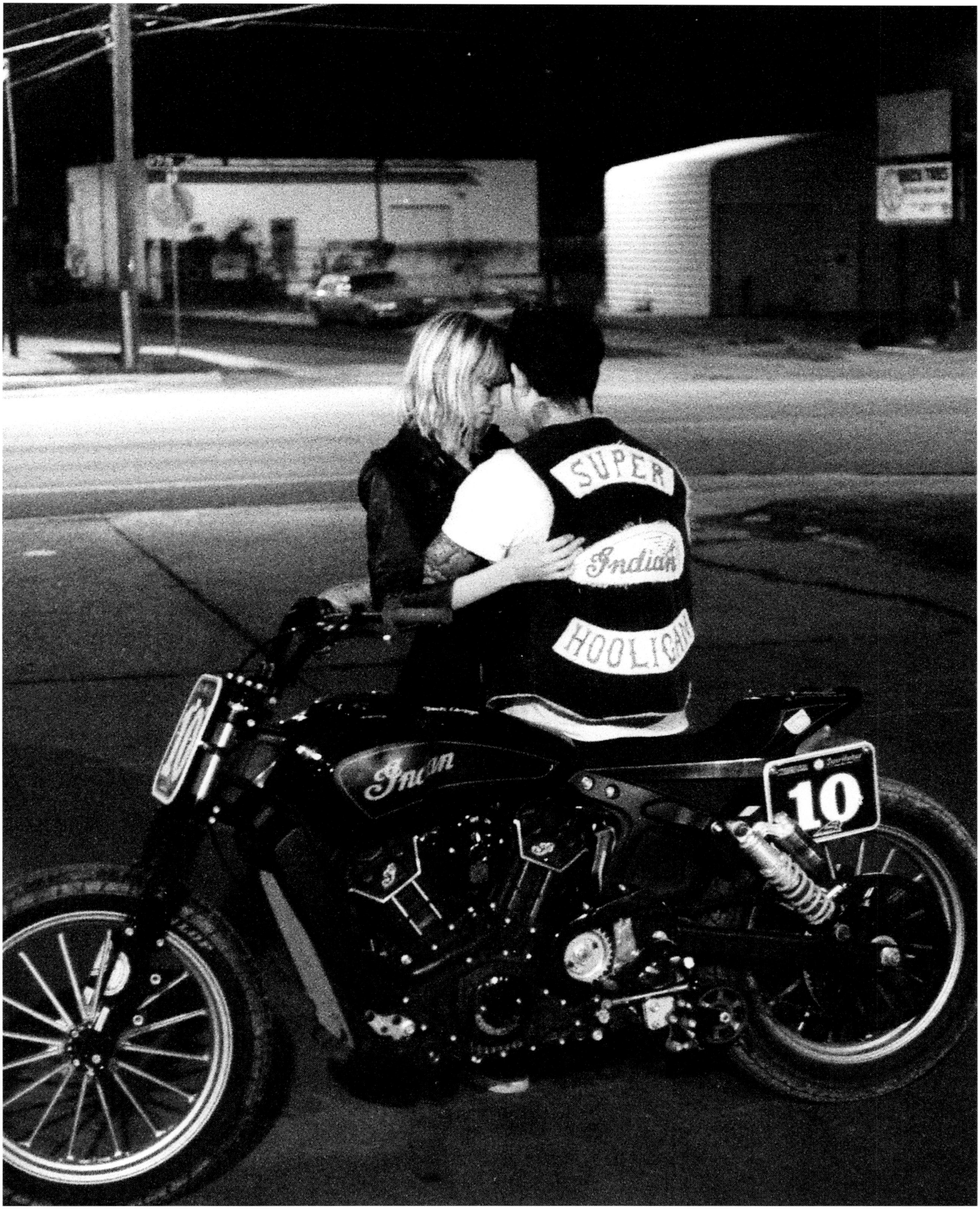
SUPER
Indian
HOOLIGANS
Indian
10

Scotty Stopnik

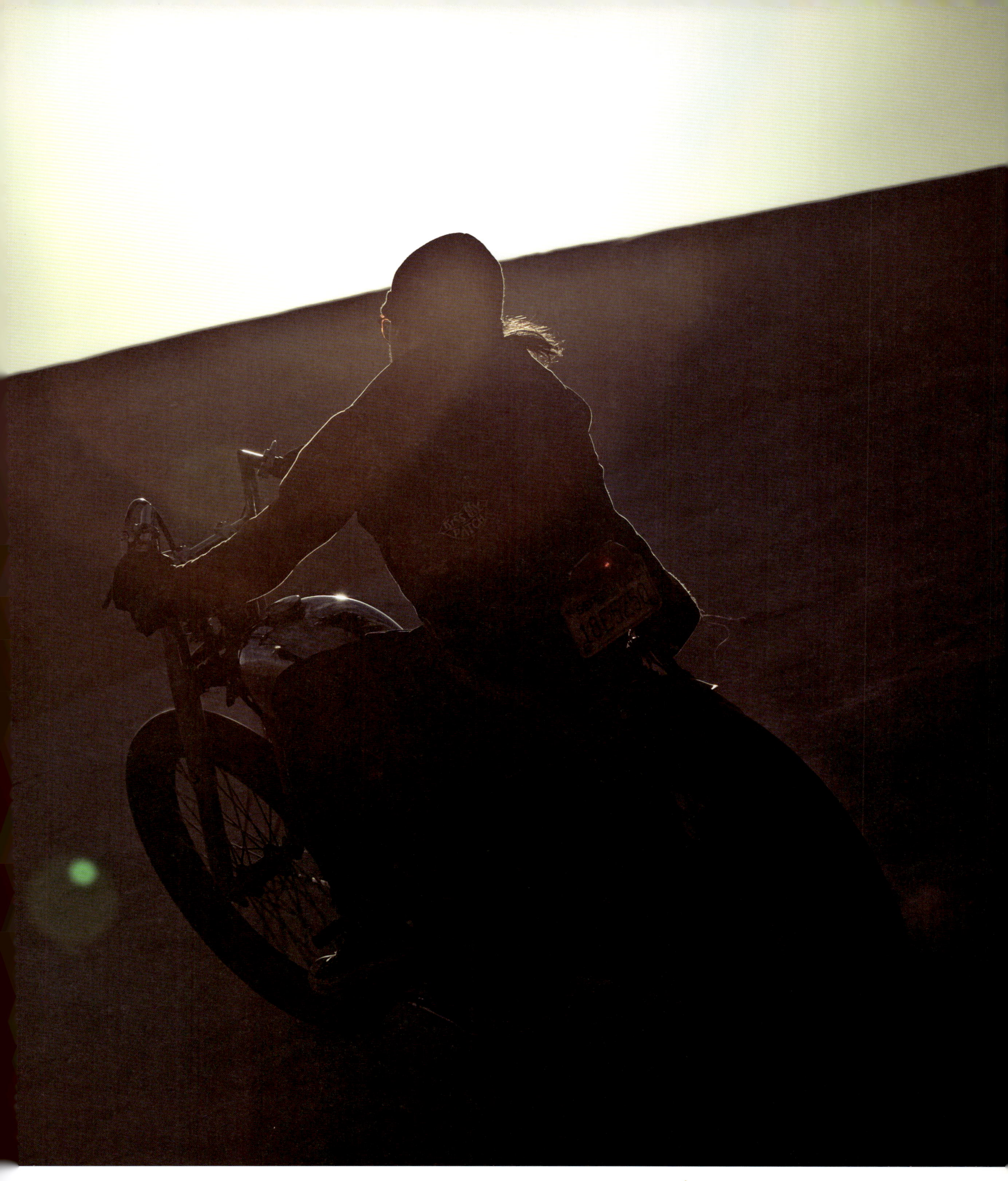

Go Takamine

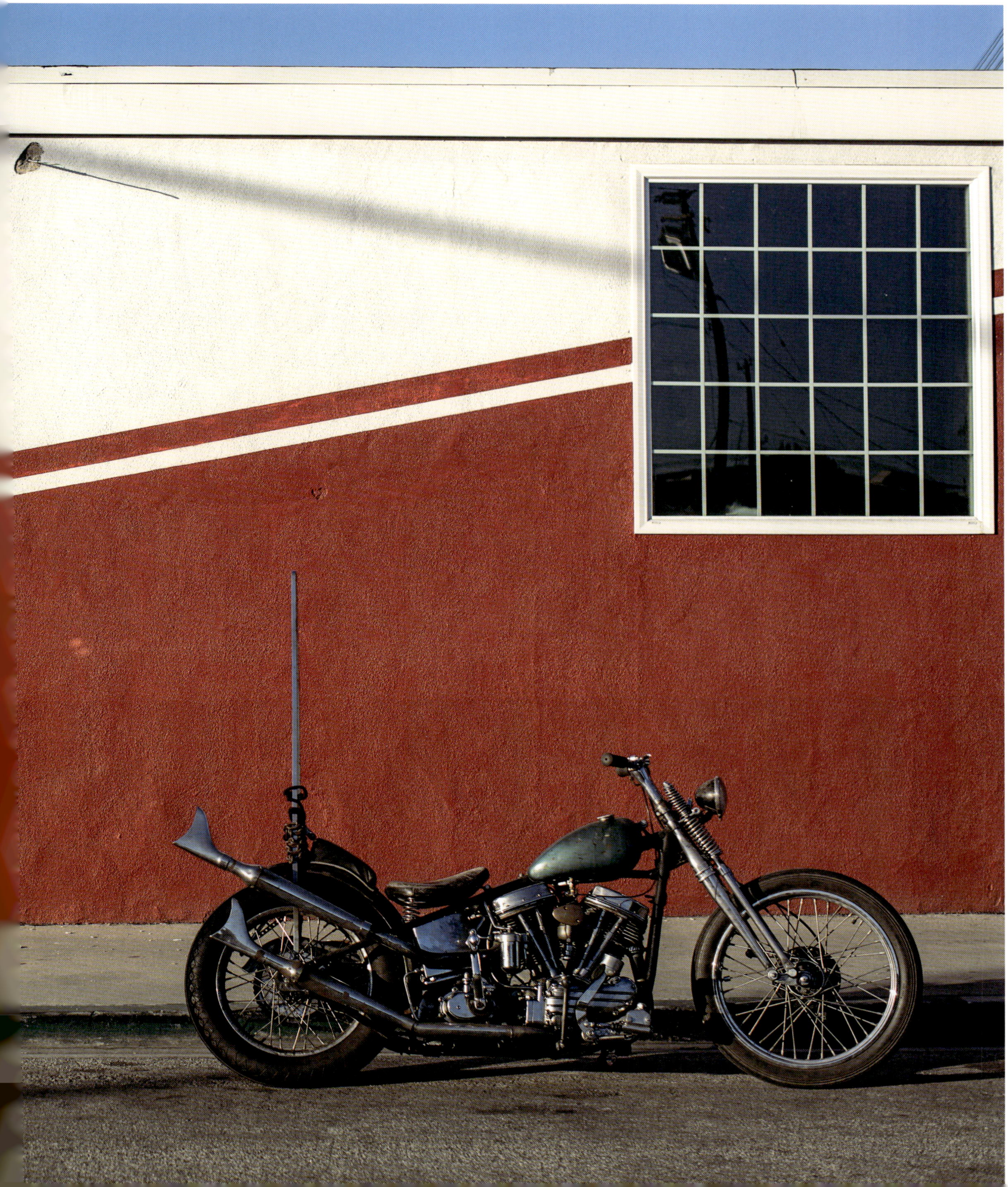

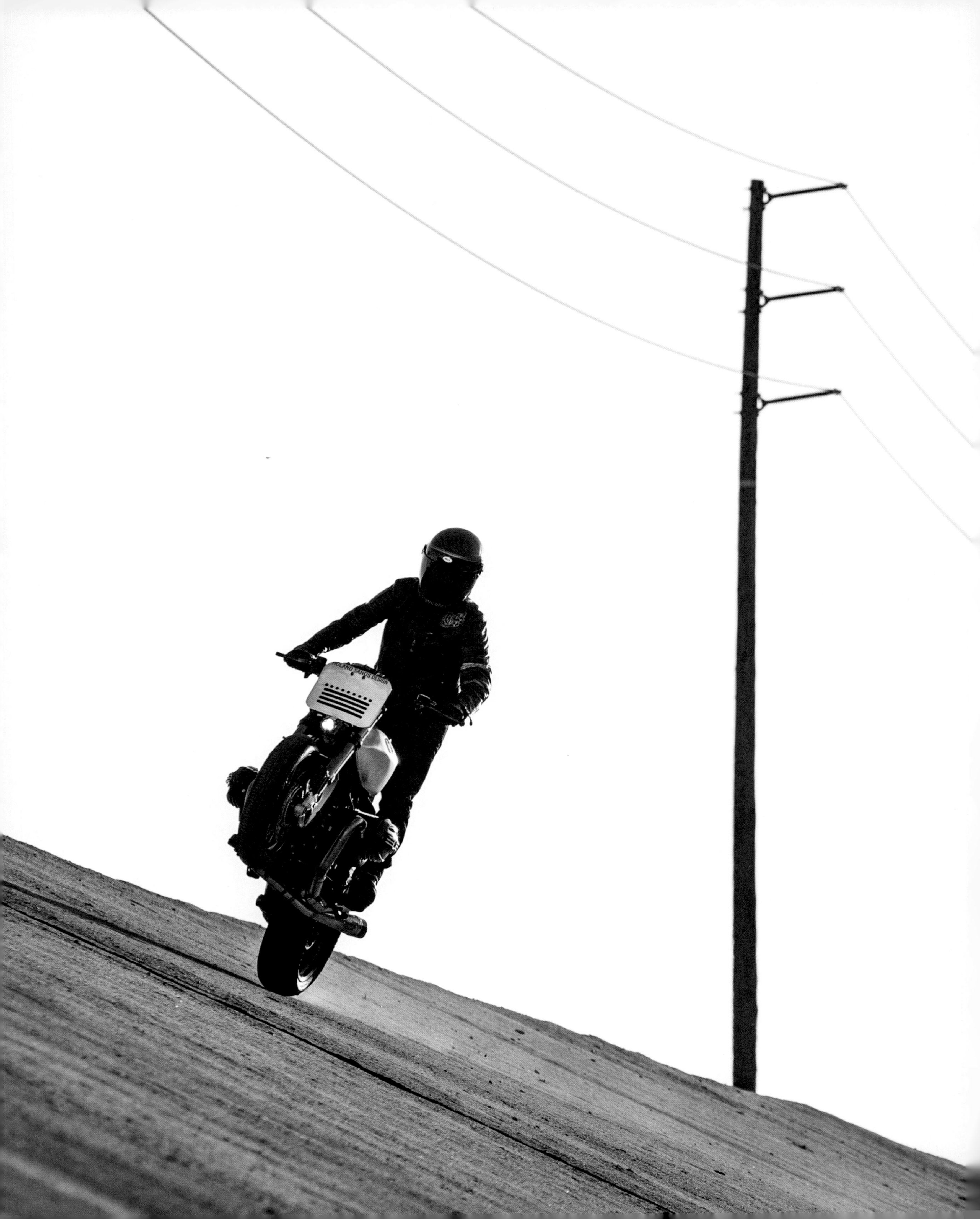

Roland Sands

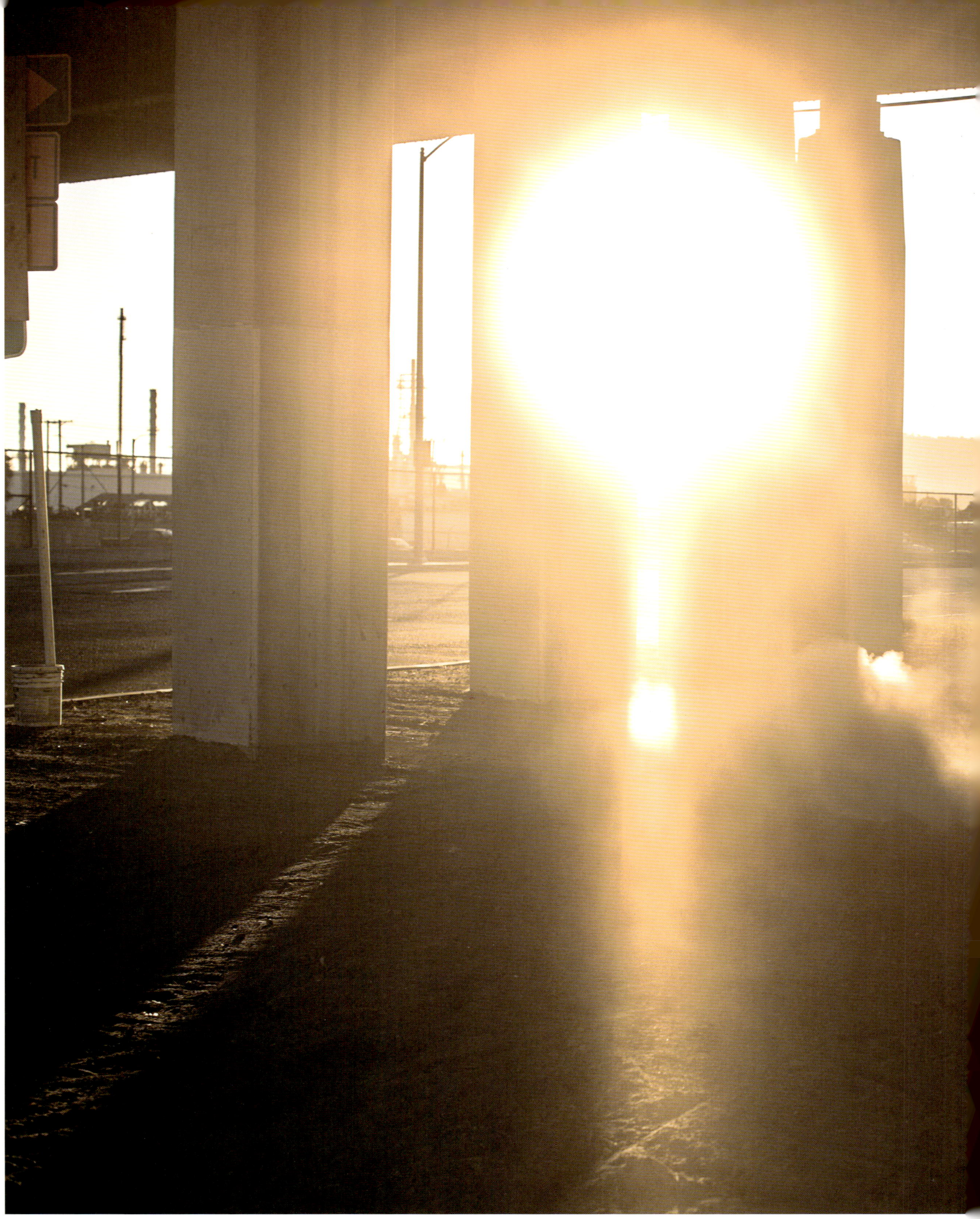

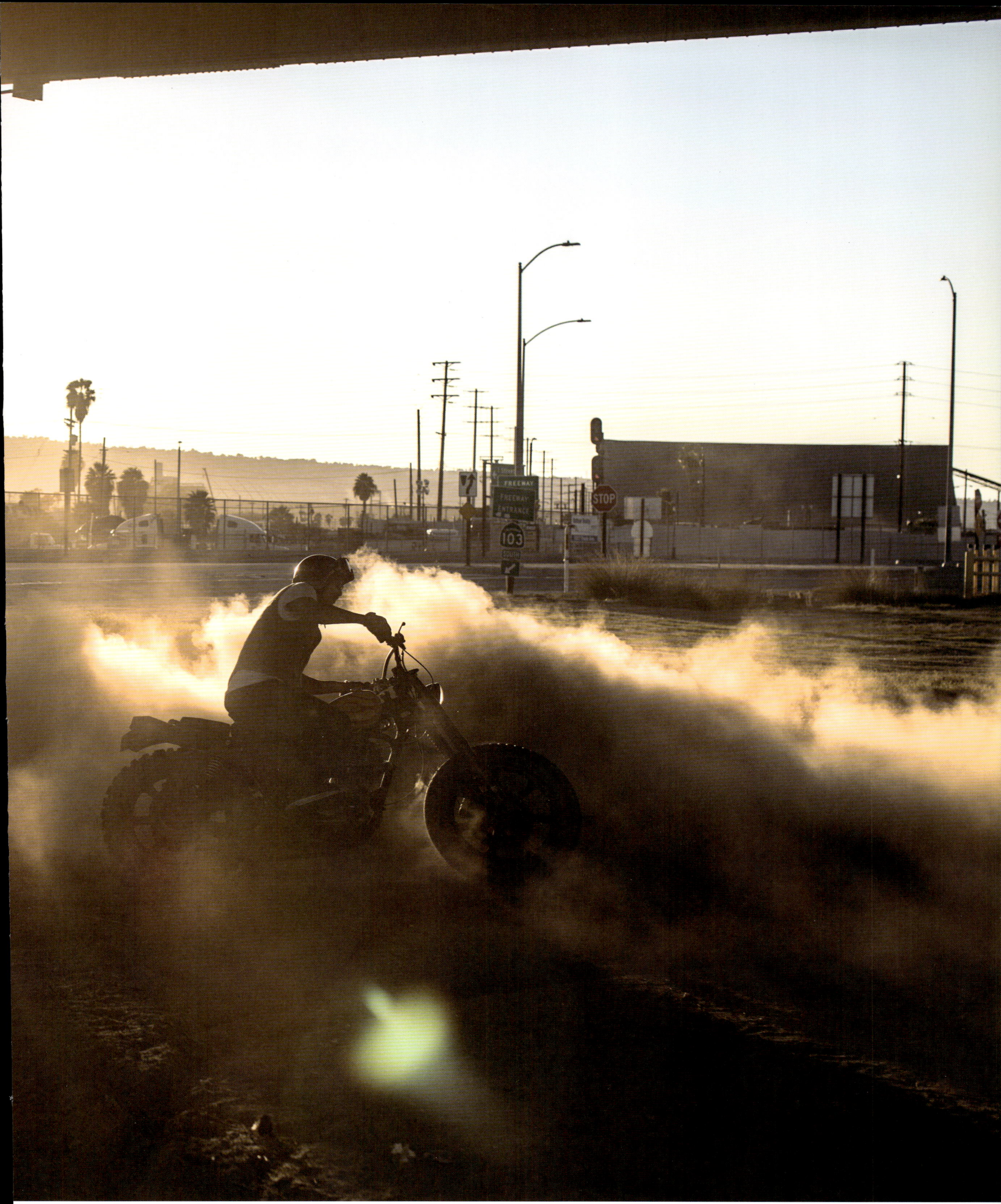
FREEWAY
FREEWAY ENTRANCE
103
STOP

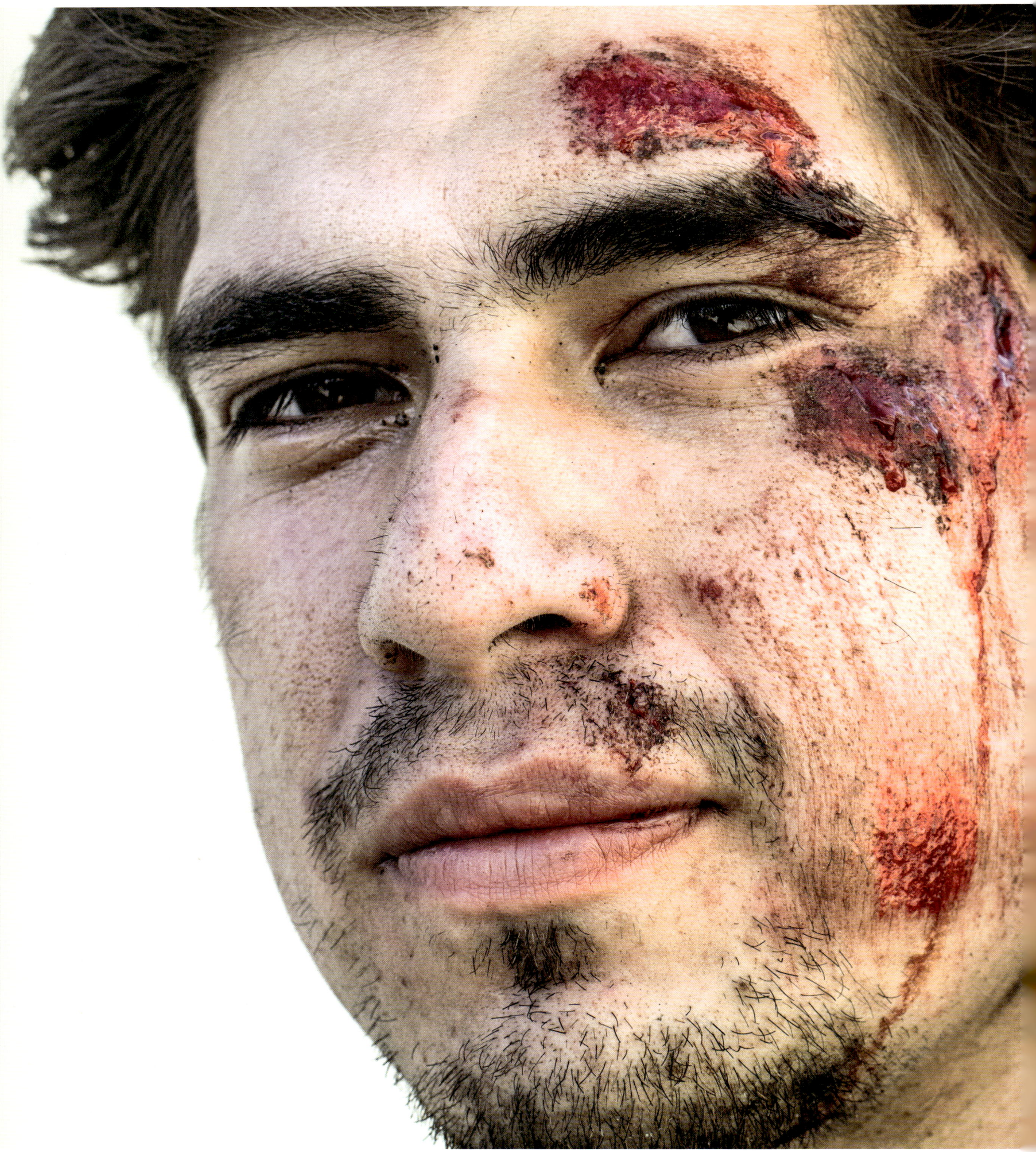

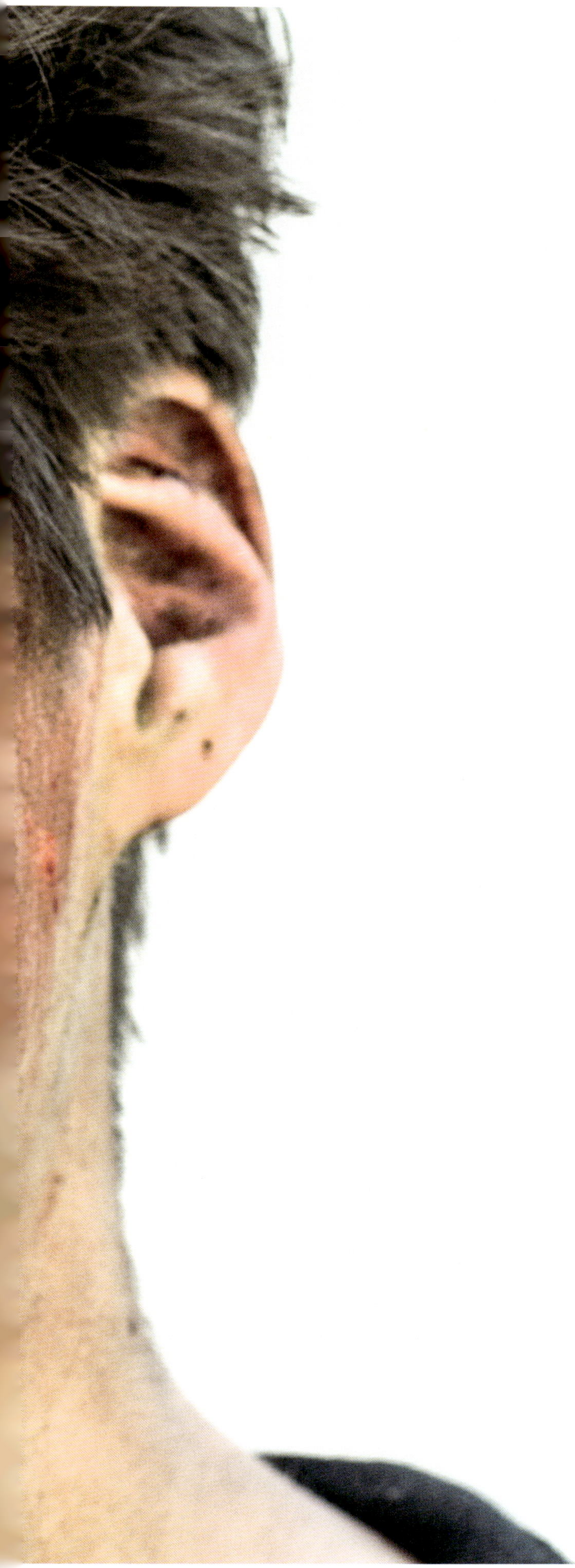

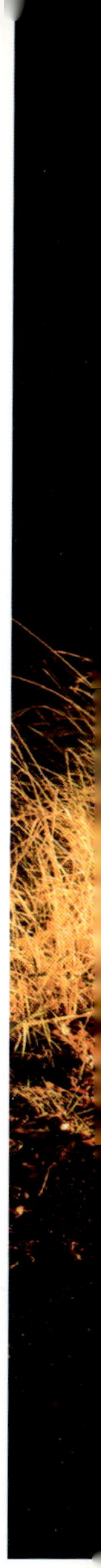

Gian Luca, Bultaco

Scott Campbell, LA River

Hell On Wheels Race

Julie Marie

Giro Motociclistico d´Italia 1923
ジロ モトチクリスティコ ディ イタリア

Ferruccio Testi

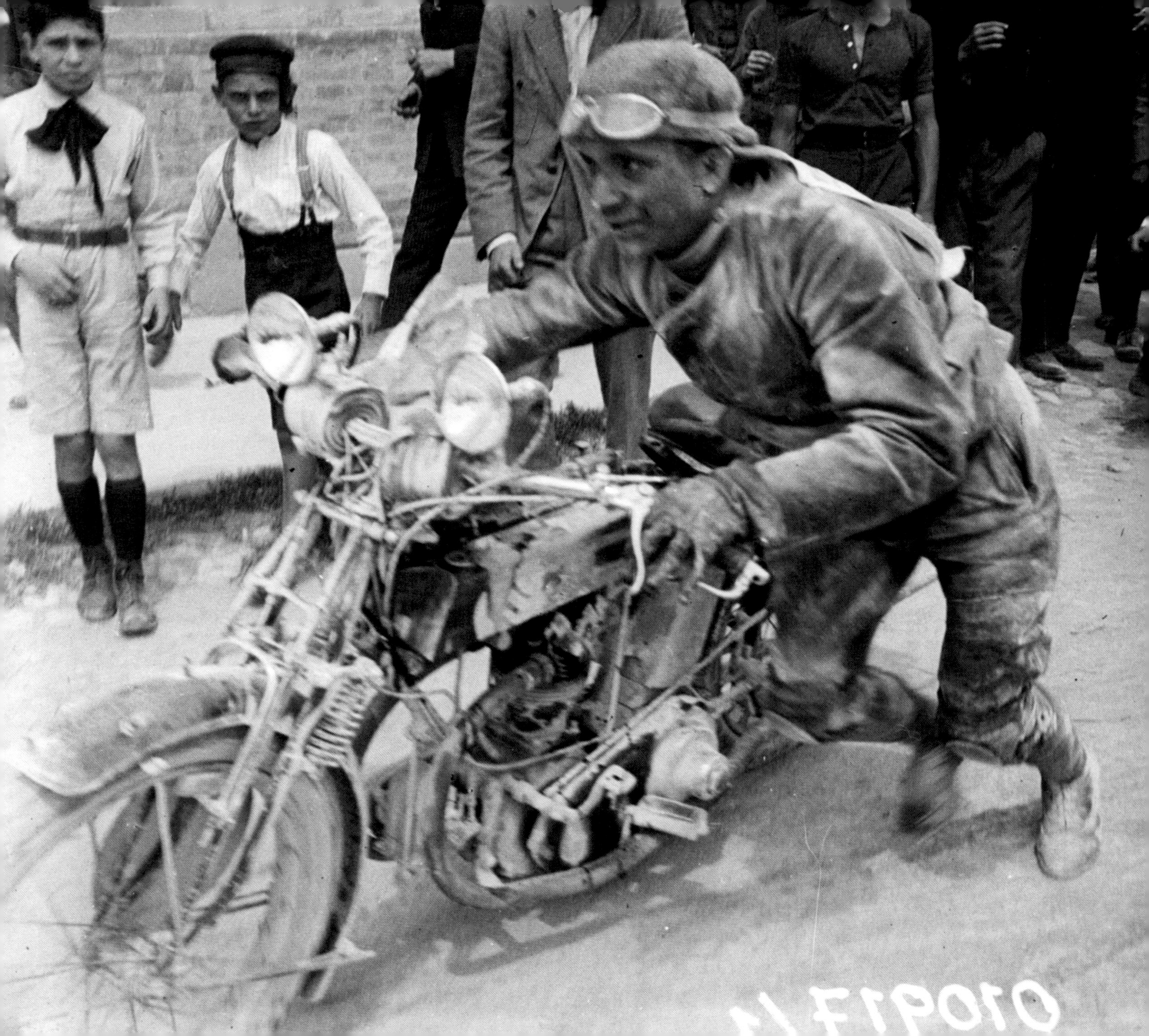

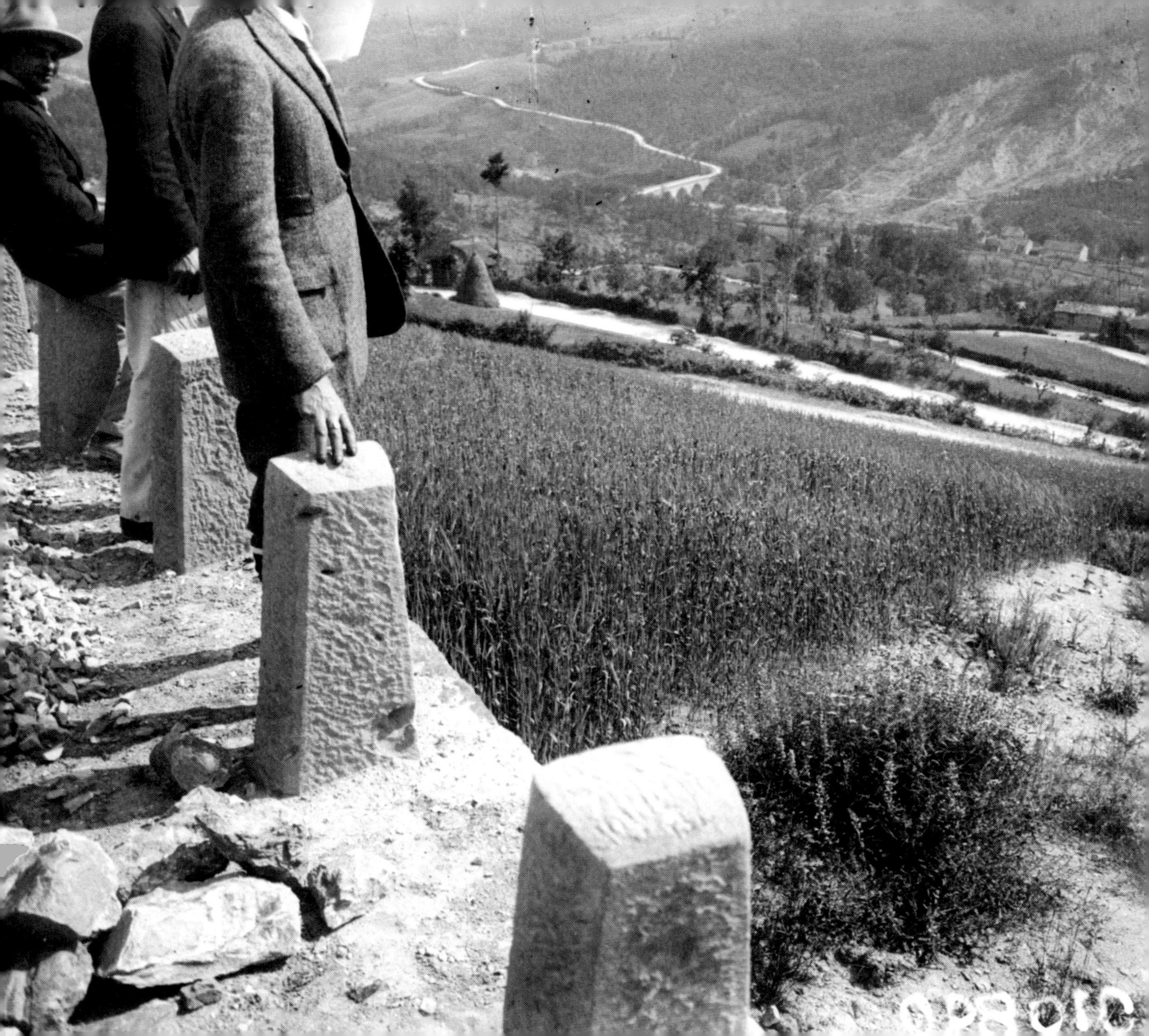

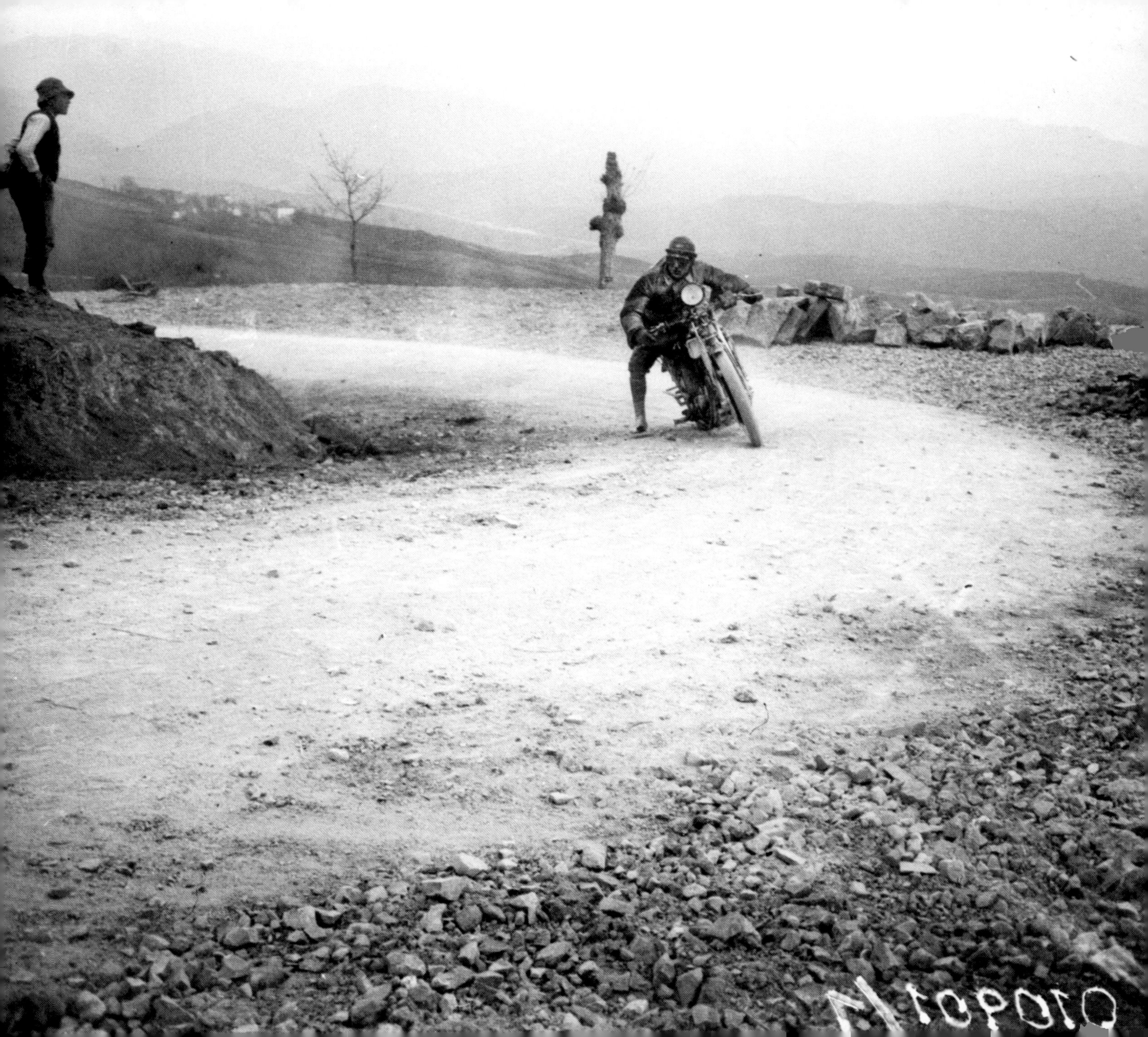

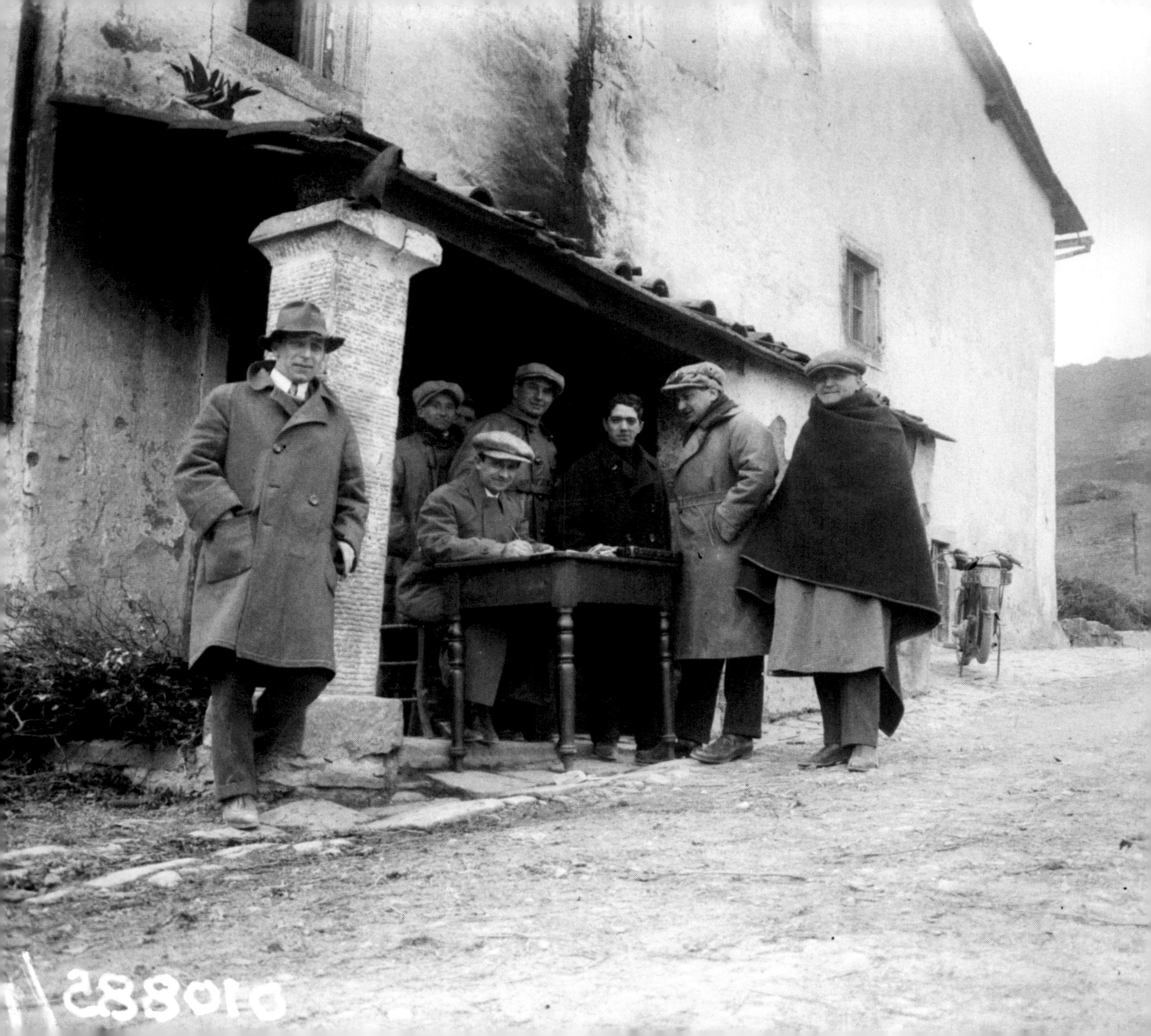

dP8010

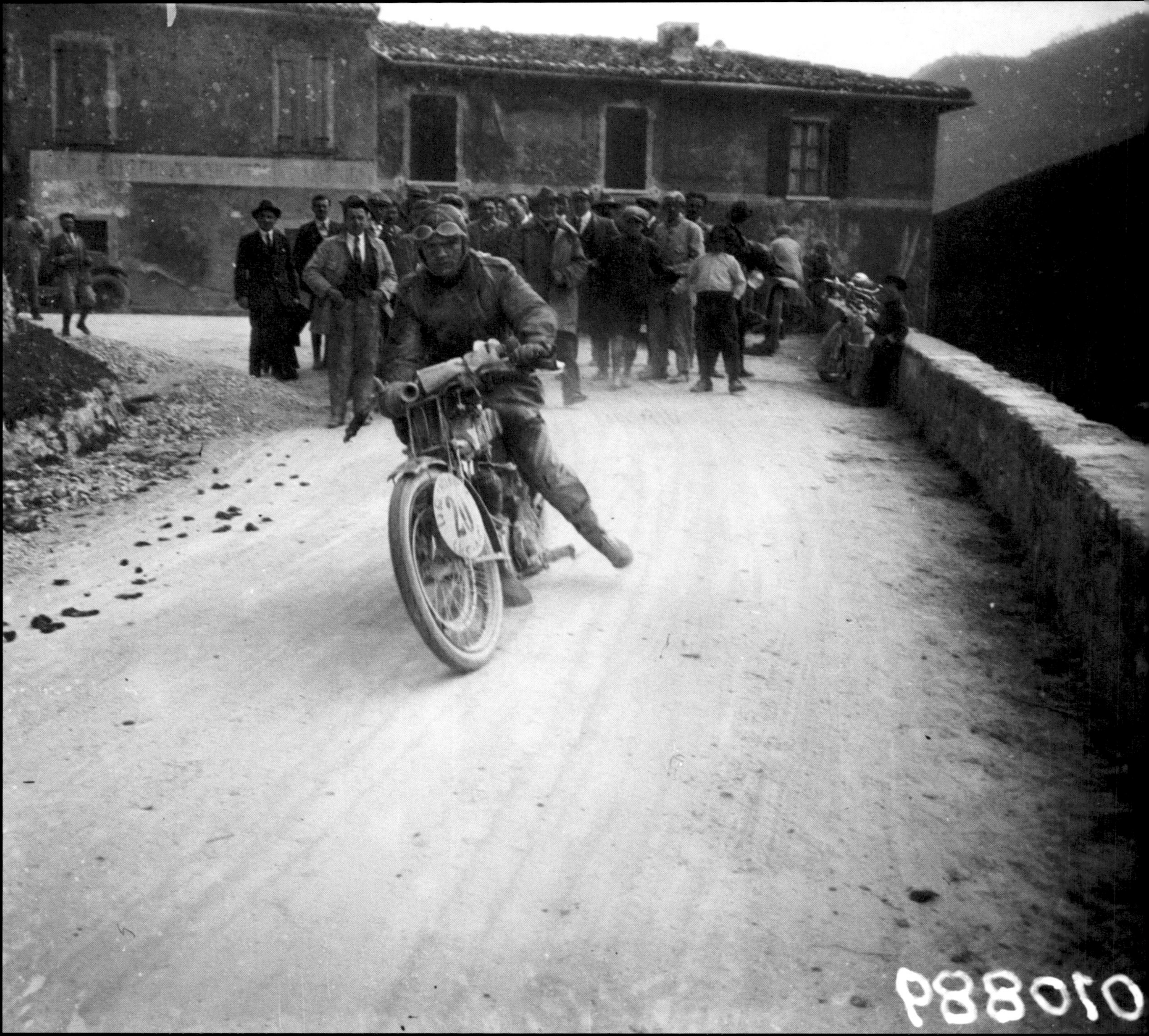

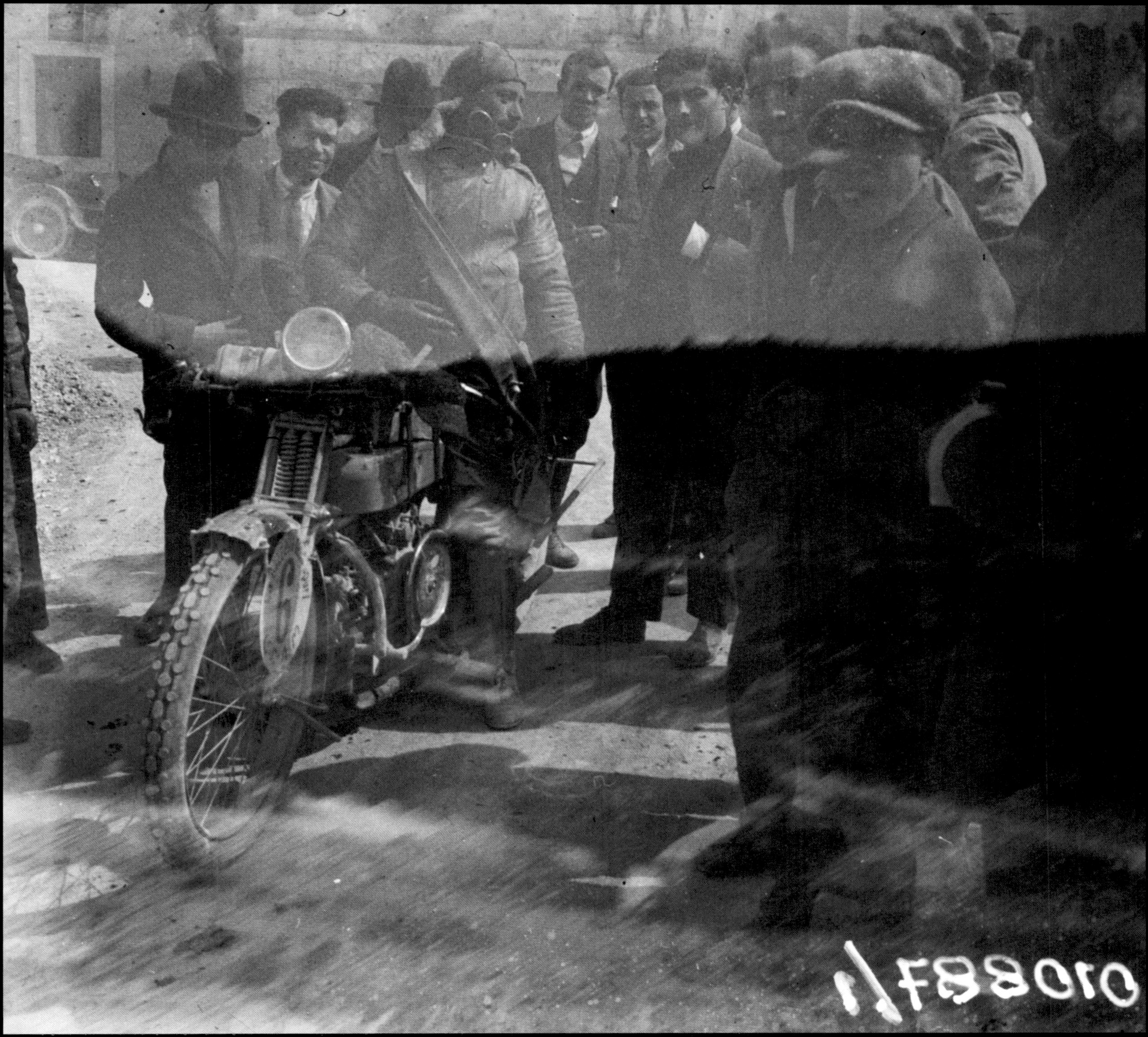

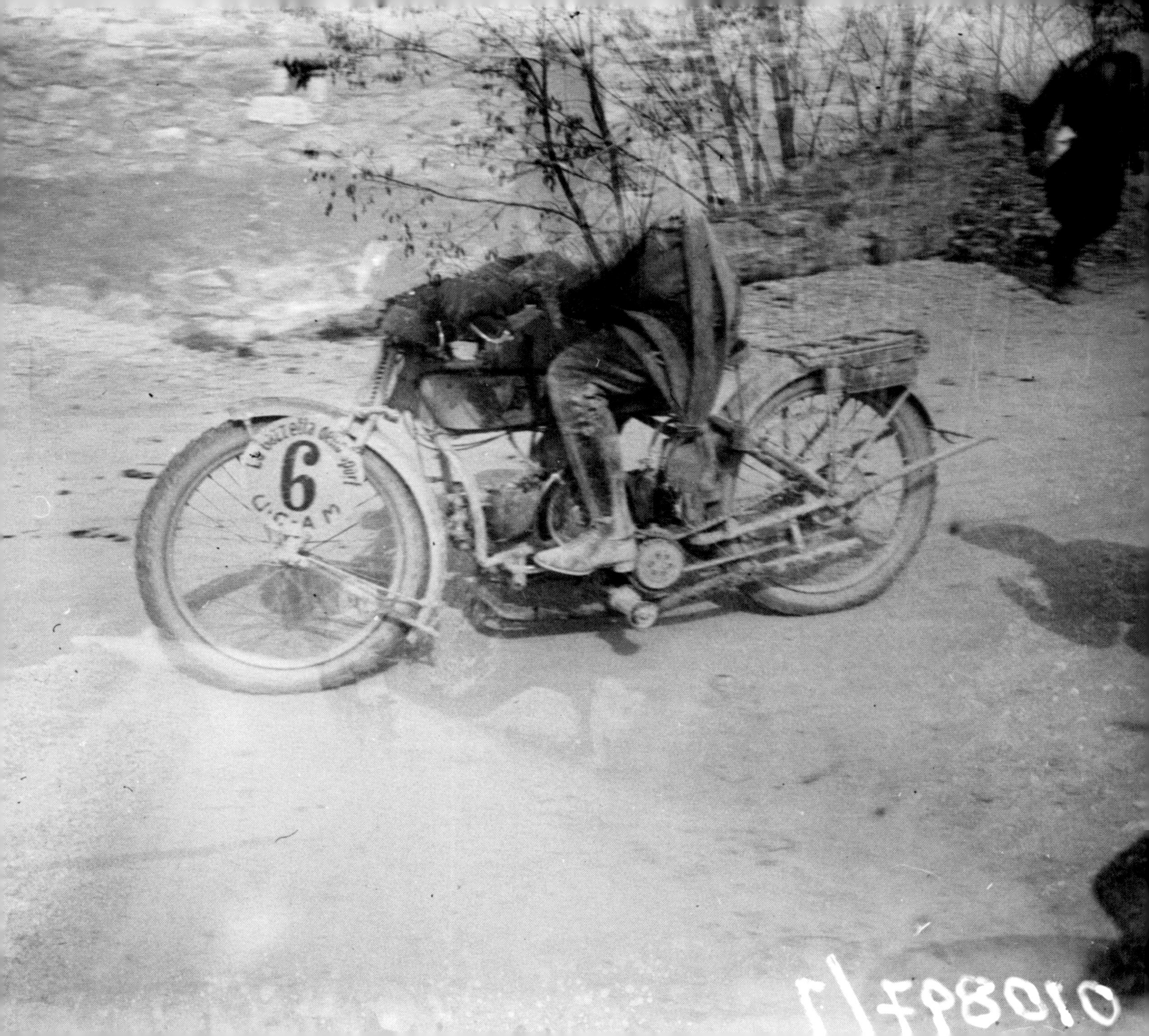
6

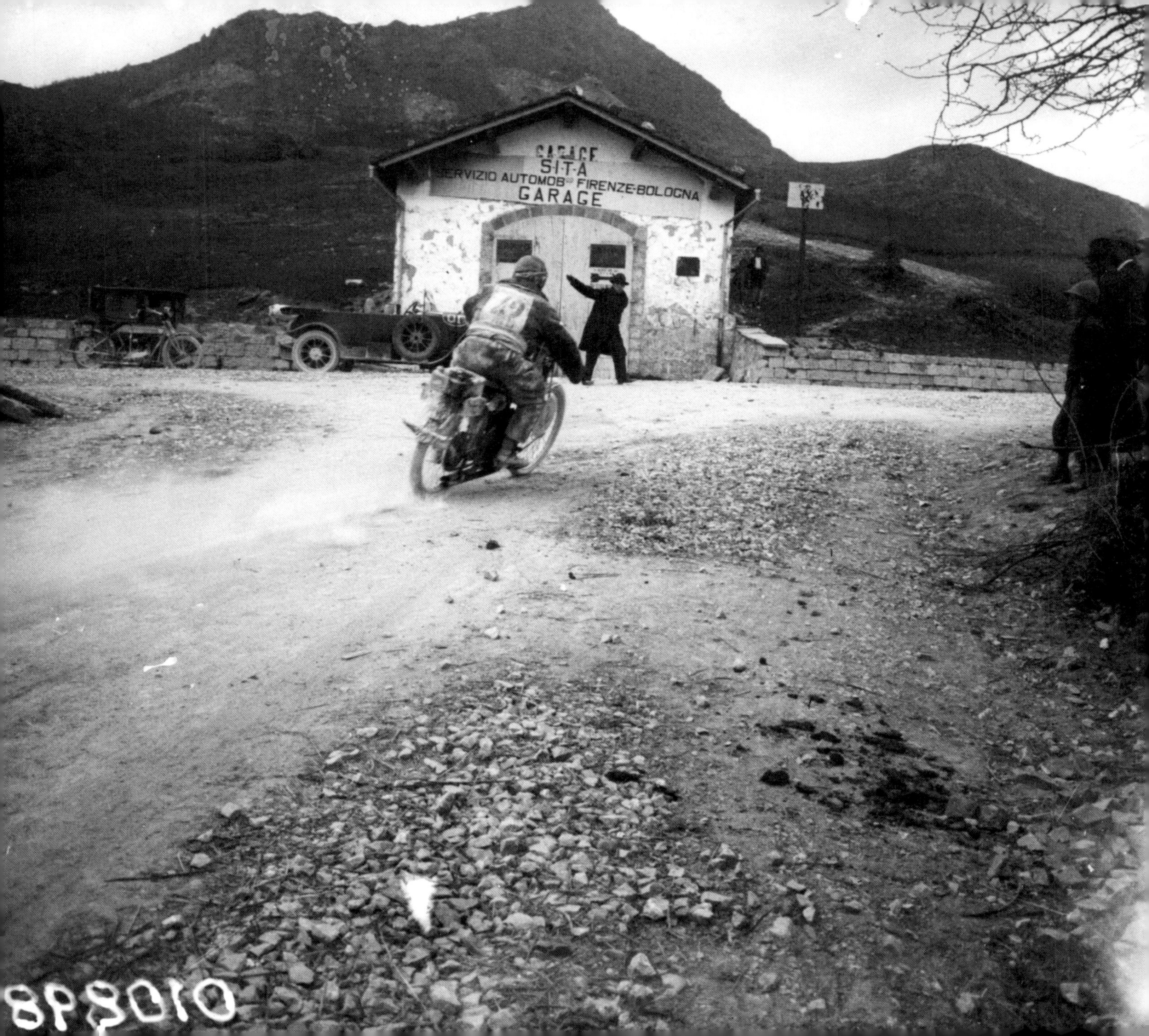
S·I·T·A
FIRENZE-BOLOGNA
GARAGE

PEI SOLI
PEDONI

popolo

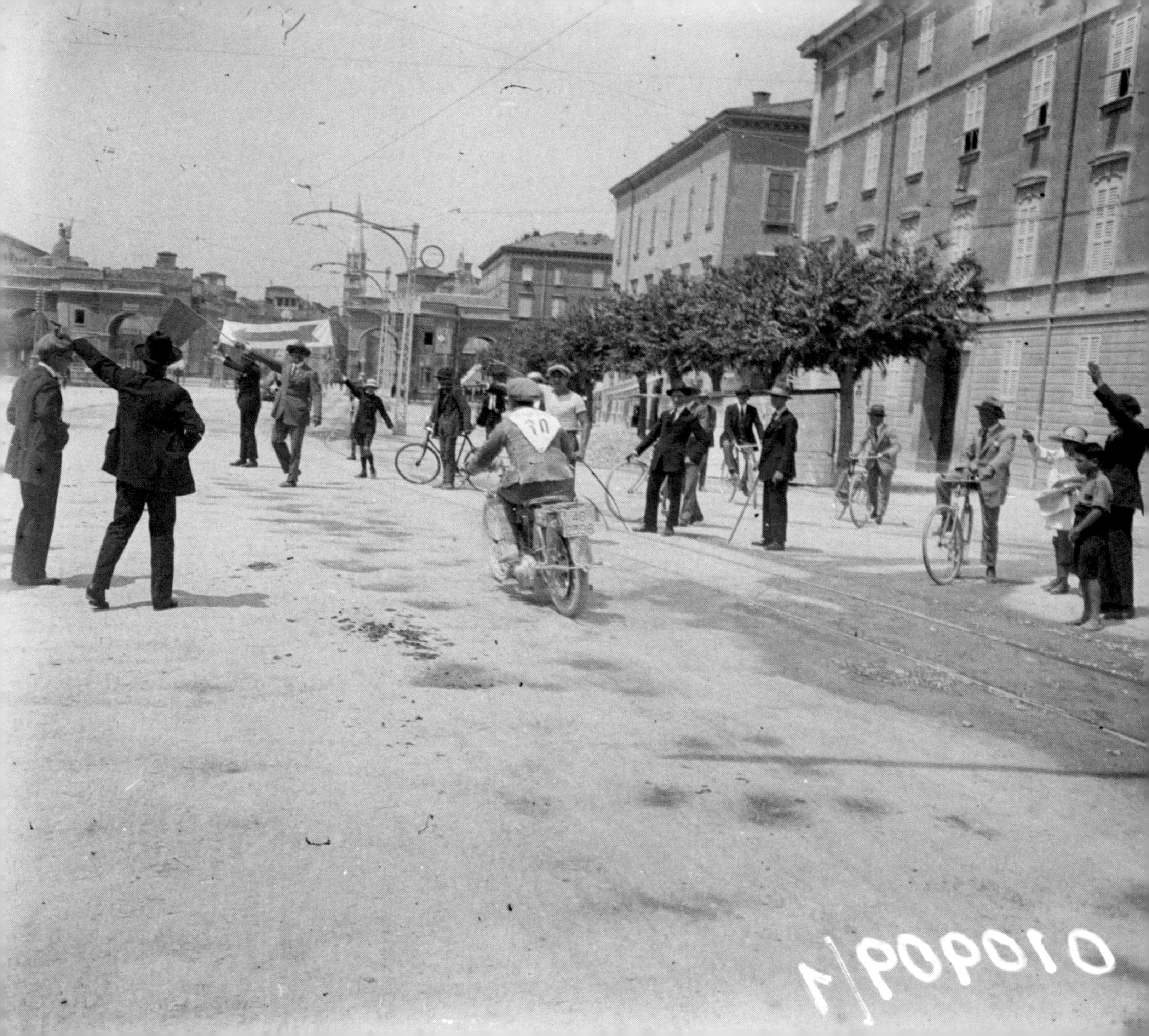

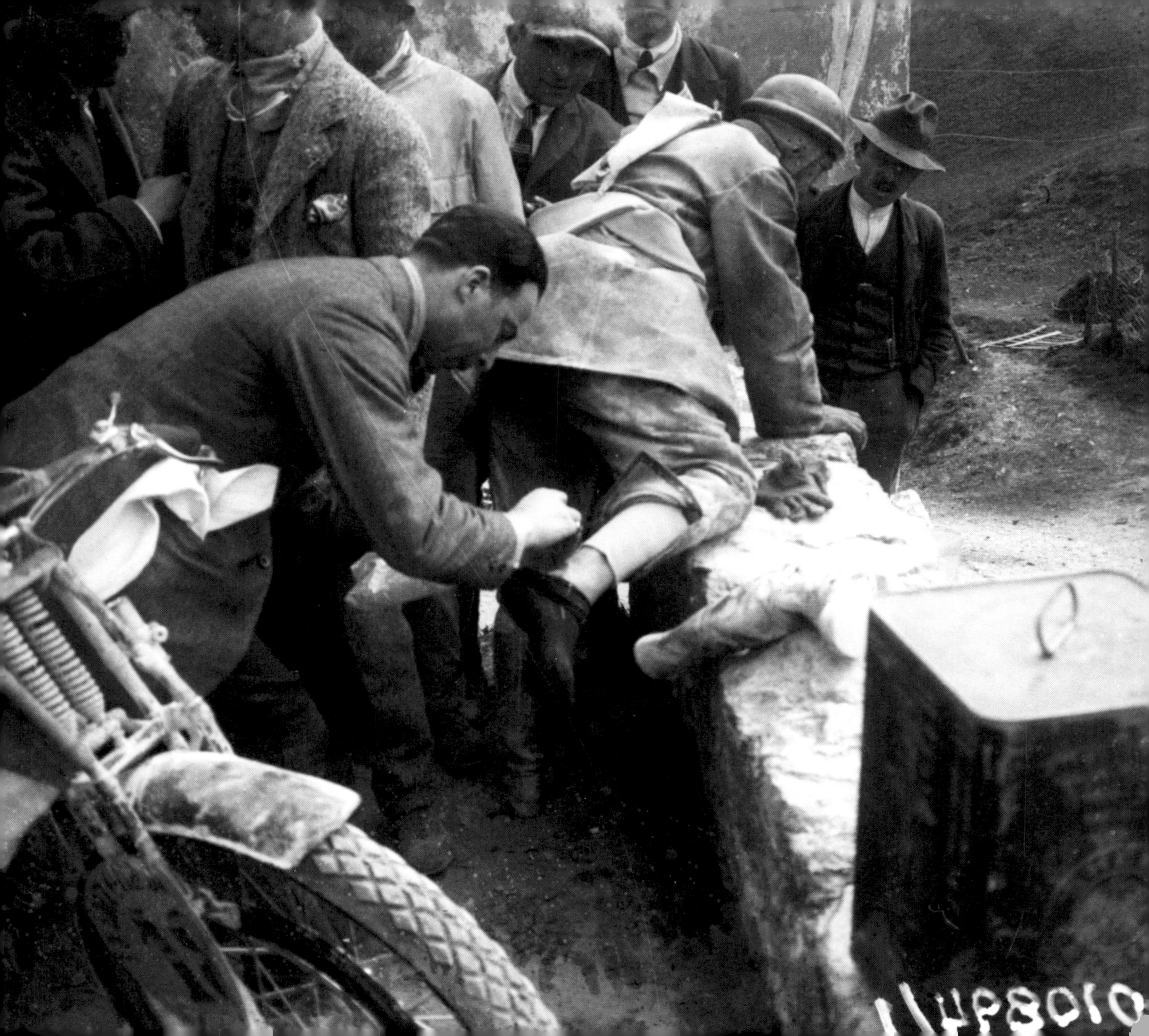

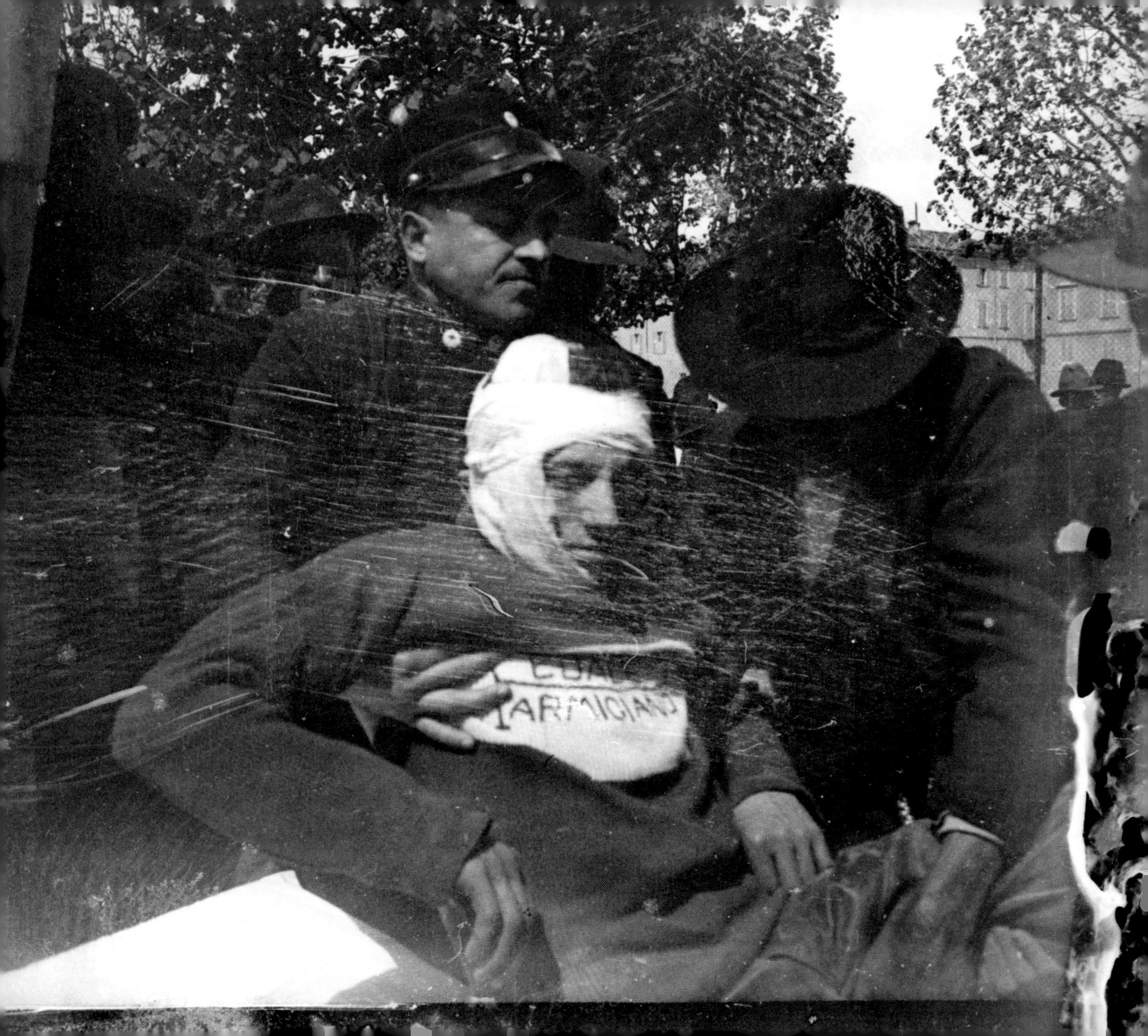

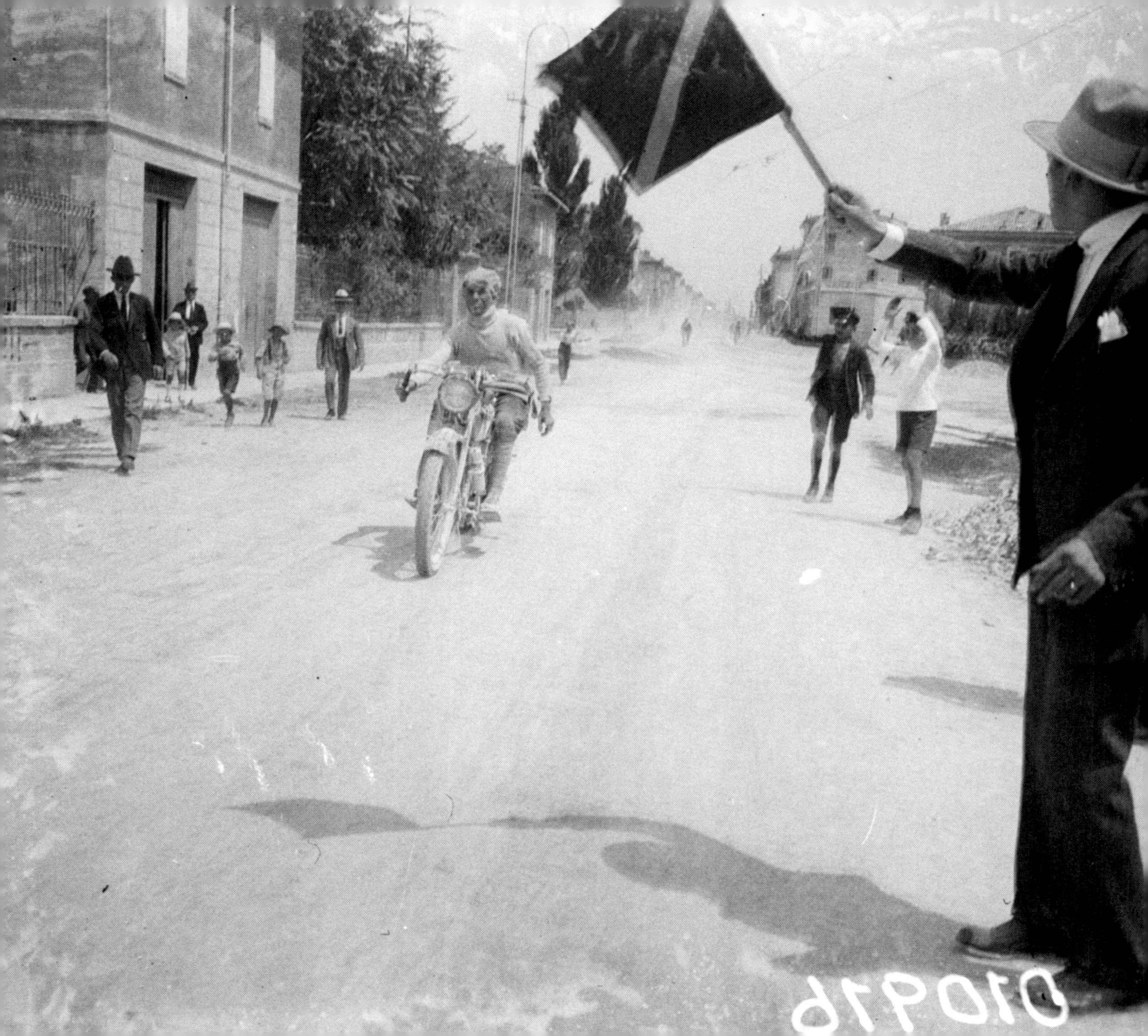

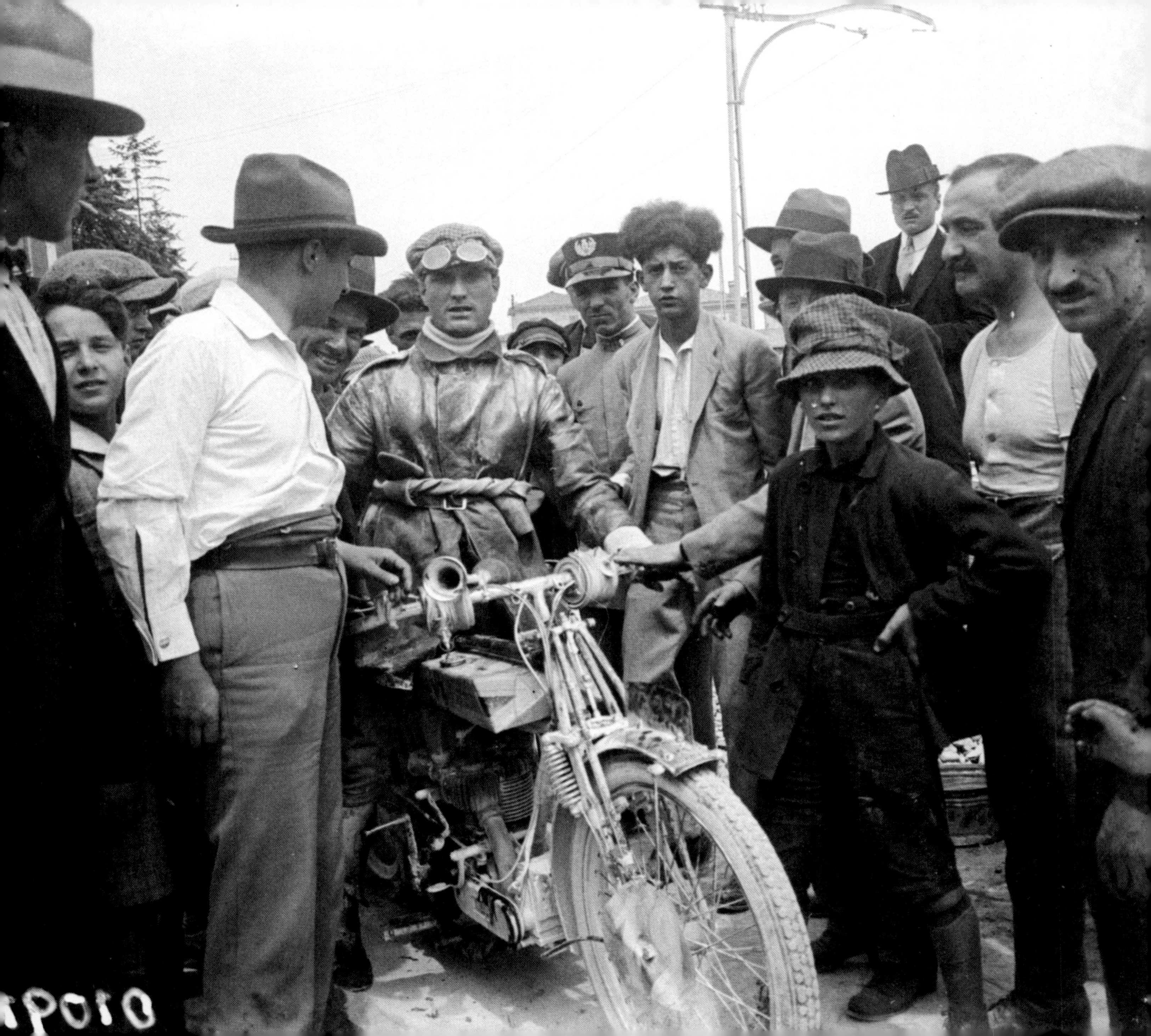

HPN, Seibersdorf
エイチ ピー エヌ、ザイバースドルフ

Hermann Köpf

from left / v.l.n.r.
Klaus Pepperl (Co-Owner of HPN)
Berthold Hauser (Ex-Teamchef BMW)
Alfred Halbfeld (Co-Owner of HPN)
Laszlo Peres (BMW)
Alexander Mayer (mechanic GS – SixDays)
Heribert Schek (Rider and Builder)
Dietmar Beinhauer (Ex-Teamchef BMW)
Eddy Hau (Rider)

Dietmar Beinhauer, Alfred Halbfeld
and Paris-Dakar-Bikes of 1980 and 1981

Marlboro
1979 DAKAR 2003
Telefónica
80
HPN
moto
SHOEI
4
MASTER

Castrol
SP ENSEIGNES
MARCOUSSIS - Tél. 69 01 59 52
MICHELIN
CLUB MOTO POLICE NATIONALE

BAJA
MONTESBLANCOS
MONROE
196

1979 DAKAR 2003
Telefónica
80

020
MOSCOW ULAN BATOR BEIJING

TELEFUNKEN
101
TELEFUNKEN

vsd
EUROPE 1
PARIS ALGER DAKAR 84
101
PARIS ALGER DAKAR 84
PASTIS 51

AURIOL
le point
BMW

AURIOL

BMW
le point
AURIOL
le point
ARCUEIL MOTOR
MICHELIN
le point
antar
101

Heribert Schek, 15 times Paris-Dakar-Rider
and Builder of this 1983 Worksbike
of Hubert Auriol talking with Klaus Pepperl (HPN)
*Heribert Schek, 15-maliger Paris-Dakar-Teilnehmer und
Erbauer dieser 1983 Werksmaschine von Hubert Auriol
im Gespräch mit Klaus Pepperl (HPN)*

Eddy Hau made 1986 on this bike place 8 at Rally Paris-Dakar
Eddy Hau belegte 1986 auf diesem Motorrad bei der Paris-Dakar den 8. Platz

elf
HELIN

oro
HPN

MICHELIN

Marlboro
Paris-Dakar

303.79
0.25
1.87

Alfred Halbfeld, Klaus Pepperl (both HPN) and former Teamchef Berthold Hauser in front of year 2000 4-valves-GS

Alfred Halbfeld, Klaus Pepperl (beide HPN) und der ehemalige Teamchef Berthold Hauser an der 4-Ventil-GS aus dem Jahr 2000

BMW Motorrad
GAULOISES
Blondes
GAS
PAN
WD 9

BMW Motorrad
GAULOISES
Blondes
GAS
BMW Motorrad
GAULOISES
Blondes
GAS

BEINHAUER
BMW

Laszlo Peres was working in BMW development department and private rider, leaning on *his* Six Days GS of 1980

Laszlo Peres war Mitarbeiter der BMW-Versuchsabteilung und Privatfahrer, hier an seiner Six Days GS aus dem Jahr 1980

Focus
フォーカス

Dimitri Coste

I started photography when I was a teenager without any intentions of turning this hobby into proper work. Most of the time, 20 plus years later I still can't figure I'm actually working on most of my shoots. Even though I take commisson jobs very seriously. As far as I remember all I can say about my photographic work is that it always needed to be connected to one of my passions, and that there's nothing I can photograph better than something I like, respect, know, love and understand. It is essential to me, and I guess helps my work to look a bit different from others on similar subjects, and hopefully soulful, true and honest.

Regarding the motorcycles in my work; what's really important and takes priority is the subject. I do not just shoot anything on 2 wheels or any random bike builder, I deeply need to photograph people I admire and respect. I do my best to avoid being fooled by fakes and wannabees. It can seem pretentious or arrogant, but that's also what makes my photos shine more than others sometimes... well I hope. I'm not craving to shoot just anything, only the right things, the genuine persons, people or bikes I feel related to, appreciate and respect. Otherwise, I'd rather be just riding, which I actually do more than shooting in the end. And that's another reason why I can't shoot just anything. I know the scenes, I know about motorcycles and I can read between lines most of the time and spot what's real from what isn't. If there's riding involved, I can't shoot people that can barely ride. I need to be impressed and shoot people that do things I can't do.

Again this might seem arrogant, but I'm just trying to be true to myself and to people who follow me and like my work. At the end of the day, I think what makes my motorcycle photos mine, is the fact that I choose my subjects and usually end up establishing some sort of a two-way relationship with them involving a common language, which is riding. And the fact that I ride, get dirty, crash sometimes and give 100 % every time, plays a role in those relationships that doesn't make me just a guy who wants a cool photo then leaves and probably will never be back unless needed. I don't lie, but I love to share... but only the good stuff with good people. It is very important to me nowadays where photography has become so easy and standing out has become so tough. I learned the old way with films, labs and countless hours in the dark when the internet did not exist and trendspotters and imitators were rare, and credibility had to be earned for real.

The aesthetics of riding positions and moves are priority. I grew up fed by action photography. Motocross, BMX and skateboarding shaped up my tastes, and those are scenes where action doesn't lie. Then all I care about is the vibe, the atmosphere and the light. Playing with light, either artificial or natural is very exciting to me and a creative tool. Regarding equipment, I play with all kinds of cameras. From medium format to digital, and can apply Sideburn's magazine famous saying »It's not what you ride, it's how you ride it.« to photography. Whatever tool is in your hands, what counts at the end is the effort, the soul and sincerity you add to make it real photography, not just another pic in a world totally flooded by images everywhere.

I shoot like I ride, following my instinct rather than the rules... but I learnt them before, which allows me to be free and embrace the spectacle.

Paris-born Dimitri Coste is a photographer and film director whose extensive work is ingrained with his immense passion for motorcycles and American culture. Always on the move, he can be found shooting action photos in the mud one day, then shooting fashion in studio another day. Both with the same enthusiasm and his very own way of looking at things. Landscapes, fashion, lifestyle or automobile, he shoots what he likes and is attached to spread and share the beauty he sees with his own photographic style, often playing with singular angles and approach of lighting and his quest for authenticity. What makes his motorcycles photos so special is that he is himself an active amateur racer, a regular of the UK vintage flat track series, he won the open twin class at the 2010 Catalina GP, is a Pikes Peak finisher and an occasional Super Hooligan racer on RSD Indian Scout. His clients are Hennessy, Persol, 100%, BMW Motorrad, Yamaha Europe, Vans, Ruby Helmets, Jerôme Dreyfuss, Isabel Marant, MGM Park, Renault Sport etc.

Ich begann als Teenager mit dem Fotografieren, ohne je daran gedacht zu haben, das Hobby zu meinem Beruf zu machen. Auch heute, zwanzig Jahre später, habe ich bei den meisten Shootings nicht das Gefühl, zu arbeiten, obwohl ich Auftragsjobs sehr ernst nehme. Seit ich mich erinnern kann, war mir das Wichtigste an meiner fotografischen Arbeit, dass sie mit einer meiner Leidenschaften verbunden sein sollte und dass es nichts gibt, das ich besser fotografieren kann, als Dinge, die ich respektiere, kenne, liebe und verstehe. Es ist essentiell für mich und ich glaube, dies ist auch der Grund dafür, dass meine Fotos sich ein bisschen unterscheiden von anderen Arbeiten mit ähnlichen Motiven. Hoffentlich vermitteln sie mehr Seele, Wahrheit und Ehrlichkeit.

Bei den Motorrädern, die ich fotografiere, ist das Motiv für mich das einzig Wichtige und hat absolute Priorität. Ich schieße nicht einfach irgendetwas auf zwei Rädern oder irgendeinen zufälligen Motorradbauer, ich muss die Menschen, die ich fotografiere bewundern und respektieren. Ich bemühe mich, nicht auf Schwindler und Blender hereinzufallen. Das mag prätentiös oder arrogant erscheinen, aber dadurch bekommen meine Bilder ihre besondere Ausstrahlung ... Hoffe ich zumindest. Ich bin nicht darauf versessen, möglichst viel zu fotografieren. Ich suche die richtigen Motive, die Originale, die echten Menschen oder Maschinen, mit denen ich mich verbunden fühle, die ich schätze und respektiere. Wäre das nicht der Fall, würde ich stattdessen lieber selber Motorrad fahren, was ich sowieso öfter tue, als zu fotografieren. Dies ist der andere Grund, warum ich nicht einfach irgendetwas fotografieren kann: Ich kenne die Szene genau, ich kenne mich mit Motorrädern aus, ich kann meistens zwischen den Zeilen lesen und erkennen, was echt ist und was nicht. Wenn es um das Thema Fahren geht, kann ich nicht einfach Leute fotografieren, die es nicht wirklich können. Die Fahrer müssen mich beeindrucken und Sachen können, die ich nicht kann.

Das klingt auch wieder ziemlich arrogant, aber ich versuche nur, mir selbst und den Menschen gegenüber, die mich und meine Arbeit verfolgen und mögen, wahrhaftig zu sein. Ich glaube, dass was meine Bilder authentisch macht, ist die Tatsache, dass ich meine Motive selbst wähle und es normalerweise schaffe, eine Art gegenseitiger Verbindung mit den Menschen durch unsere gemeinsame Sprache, die des Fahrens, aufzubauen. Und die Tatsache, dass ich selber fahre, dreckig werde, auch hin und wieder stürze, aber immer hundert Prozent gebe, spielt eine wichtige Rolle in dieser Verbindung. Ich bin dann nicht nur der Typ, der ein einfach cooles Foto will, anschließend abhaut und wahrscheinlich nie wieder kommt, sofern er nicht noch einmal gebraucht wird. Ich lüge nicht, aber ich liebe es, mich auszutauschen und zu teilen … Aber nur hochwertige Bilder und mit anderen guten Fotografen. Das ist sehr wichtig für mich, nachdem das Fotografieren heutzutage so einfach geworden ist und es immer schwieriger wird, sich aus der Masse herauszuheben. Ich habe noch die alte Art des Fotografierens gelernt, mit Filmen, Laboren und endlosen Stunden in der Dunkelkammer. Das Internet existierte noch nicht, Trendscouts und Nachahmer waren rar und Glaubwürdigkeit musste hart verdient werden.

Die Ästhetik der Fahrpositionen und Bewegungen haben Priorität für mich. Ich bin mit der Action-Fotografie groß geworden. Motocross, BMX und Skateboard fahren haben mich geprägt. Das sind die Szenen, in denen die Action echt ist. Darüber hinaus sind mir die Stimmung, die Atmosphäre und das Licht extrem wichtig. Mit dem Licht zu spielen, egal ob künstliches oder natürliches Licht, ist sehr spannend und ein kreatives Werkzeug für mich. Was die Ausstattung angeht, spiele ich mit allen Arten von Kameras, von Mittelformat- bis zu Digitalkameras. Für mich kann man den bekannten Ausspruch des Sideburn Magazines auch auf die Fotografie anwenden: »Es kommt nicht darauf an, was du fährst, sondern wie du es fährst.« Egal welches Werkzeug du in der Hand hältst, das was am Ende zählt, ist die Mühe, die Seele und die Ernsthaftigkeit, die du in eine Fotografie investierst, damit es nicht nur ein weiteres Bild in einer von Bildern überfluteten Welt wird.

Ich fotografiere wie ich fahre. Ich folge eher meinem Instinkt, als den Regeln … Aber bevor ich mich von den Regeln befreien und mich voll auf das Spektakel einlassen konnte, musste ich sie erst lernen.

Der in Paris geborene Dimitri Coste ist Fotograf und Regisseur, dessen umfangreiche Arbeit stark verbunden ist mit seiner großen Passion für Motorräder und die amerikanische Kultur. Immer unterwegs, kann er heute Action Fotos im Schlamm machen und morgen ein Fashion Shooting im Studio haben. Beides mit dem gleichen Enthusiasmus und seiner ganz eigenen besonderen Sicht auf die Dinge. Landschaft, Mode, Lifestyle oder Motorsport, er fotografiert, was er liebt und will die Schönheit, die er sieht, durch seine ganz eigene Arbeitsweise vermitteln und mit anderen teilen. Dafür spielt er mit besonderen Blickwinkeln und Lichteinstellungen, immer auf der Suche nach Authentizität. Was seine Motorradfotos so besonders macht, ist, dass er selbst aktiv Amateurrennen fährt. Er ist regelmäßiger Teilnehmer der UK Oldtimer Flat Track Serie, hat die offene Klasse für Zweizylinder Maschinen beim Catalina GP 2010 gewonnen, ist beim Pikes Peak Rennen ins Ziel gekommen und nimmt hin und wieder am Super Hooligan Rennen auf einer RSD Indian Scout teil. Zu seinen Kunden gehören Hennessy, Persol, 100%, BMW Motorrad, Yamaha Europe, Vans, Ruby Helmets, Jerome Dreyfuss, Isabel Marant, MGM Park, Renault Sport und andere.

Giro Motociclistico d´Italia 1923

ジロ モトチクリスティコ ディ イタリア

Ferruccio Testi (1882–1958)

The cameras were made of wood and had cloth bellows. Instead of films, glass plates were used. This equipment was packed onto the back of the bike and was taken everywhere on and off roads and tracks all over Italy, which was still an agricultural country. Ferruccio Testi was born in 1882 in Modena. After completing studies as a pharmacist he spent two months in the USA and brought back 200 photos, which were much admired at the time. He was able to make his hobby into a profession and became a reporter for the most widely read newspapers in the country for whom he was mainly involved in sport reporting. He was an active member of the soccer and horse racing clubs in his home city, but was even more interested in car and bike racing as well as opera. He travelled extensively on his English Triumph and made friends with all the great figures in motor sport, many of whom used to meet for lunch on Mondays at Testis home. Ferruccio Testi began photography in 6×9 cm negative format with a Contessa Nettel and, later, with a Zeiss Super Ikonta. In the thirties he continued to use glass plates for some time before moving on to negative film. Ferruccio Testi died in 1958. His life's work has survived until today and, until now, has only featured in automobile literature.

In April 1923 on Easter Monday, 53 motor cycle racers gathered in Bologna to take part in the *Giro Motociclistico d'Italia*. In 4 days they had to ride 2500 kilometers including timed circuit racing and hill climbing with long stretches between. The poor condition of the roads caused more problems than the races themselves. As well as suffering repeated technical breakdowns, riders regularly fell off their bikes, often because of exhaustion. Ferruccio Testi rode with them and photographed their trials and successes. Guido Mentasti (Moto Guzzi 500) was the first of a total of seven competitors to cross the finishing line. His average speed was 49,3 km/h. Aristide Fergnani (Indian 1000) finished in second place.

Die Kameras besaßen Gehäuse aus Holz und Balge aus Textilgewebe, statt Filmen wurden Glasplatten belichtet. Diese Ausrüstung, auf dem Motorrad fest verpackt, war dabei auf allen Reisen, über Stock und Stein, auf Pisten und Pfaden quer durch das noch bäuerlich geprägte Italien. Ferruccio Testi kam 1882 in Modena zur Welt, nach dem Abschluss eines Pharmazie-Studiums reiste er 1912 für zwei Monate in die USA und brachte 200 viel bewunderte Fotos mit. Er konnte sein Hobby zum Beruf machen und wurde als Reporter für die größten Zeitungen des Landes, vorwiegend auf dem Sportsektor tätig. Als Funktionär war er in den Fußball- und Pferderenn-Vereinen seiner Heimatstadt aktiv, doch mehr noch interessierten ihn Auto- und Motorradrennen sowie die Oper. Auf seiner englischen Triumph kam er viel herum und schloss Bekanntschaften mit allen Größen des Motorsports, die nicht selten auch zum montäglichen Mittagstisch im Hause Testi erschienen. Fotografiert hat Ferruccio Testi zunächst im Negativformat 6 × 9 cm mit einer Contessa Nettel, später mit einer Zeiss Super Ikonta. In den 1930er-Jahren verwendete er noch lange Glasplatten bevor er den Wechsel zu Negativfilmen vollzog. Ferruccio Testi verstarb 1958, sein komplettes Werk blieb jedoch bis heute erhalten und ist bisher lediglich in Automobilbüchern präsent.

Im April 1923, genauer gesagt am Ostermontag, versammelten sich in Bologna 53 Motorrad-Rennfahrer zum *Giro Motociclistico d´Italia*. Innerhalb von vier Tagen galt es eine Strecke von 2 500 km zurückzulegen, bestehend aus Rundstrecken- und Bergwertungen mit Zeitmessung sowie Verbindungsetappen. Die schlechten Straßenverhältnisse forderten wesentlich mehr Tribut als die einzelnen Rennen, neben zahlreichen technischen Defekten waren Stürze – oft aufgrund von Erschöpfung – an der Tagesordnung. Ferruccio Testi fuhr mit und hielt Erfolge wie Dramen im Bild fest. Der Schnellste der sieben ins Ziel gekommenen Fahrer war mit einer Durchschnittsgeschwindigkeit von 49,3 km/h Guido Mentasti (Moto Guzzi 500) vor Aristide Fergnani (Indian 1000).

Text: Stefan Knittel

HPN, Seibersdorf
エイチ ピー エヌ、ザイバースドルフ

Hermann Köpf

In a former pub in a village with 300 inhabitants in the southeastern corner of Bavaria at the beginning of the early eighties Alfred Halbfeld, Klaus Pepperl and Michael Neher set up shop and began to build pure offroad machines in a former stable. The *N* in the company name *HPN Motorradtechnik* left the company after a few years, but the products which Halbfeld and Pepperl build there have achieved cult status among the fans of the white and blue badge. Their stores, workshop and their small showroom are full with the finest components and with motorcycles, which have made history.

It is a rainy winter day for a reunion of a few grey-haired men in this historic place. Many years have gone by as they greet each other in the courtyard – as old friends do – they tell of their experiences together. You listen attentively to their stories of their glory days.

One of the circle of friends, Laszlo Peres, was a driving force in the development of offroad competition machines by the Munich manufacturer even before their prestigious Paris-Dakar successes. At the introduction of an offroad sport class for machines of over 750cc capacity in 1977, he built together with two colleagues in the BMW development department the Six Days GS which weighed in at just 124kg and on which he was vice-champion in the amateur class one year later.

In 1979 the legendary Paris-Dakar was run for the first time and, in the second year after its introduction the Bavarians started with their own Boxer-Team. One of today's guests this afternoon at the home of HPN, Dietmar Beinhauer, was their team manager at the time. He built the first *Les Concessionnaires* machines together with a friend in his garage and contributed to the resounding success of his employer with the drivers Auriol and Fenouil, when Auriol won their first overall victory on the *Le Point* in 1981.

Another guest from the Allgäu region is the 14-times German Offroad and double European Champion, who won Gold 12 times at the Six Days World Championship. When the regulations deemed him too old after 25 years of competition he then competed a further 15 times in the Paris-Dakar. At the age of 84, the charismatic Heribert Schek still competes today in Classic Enduros and enlivens these events with his presence. In 1983 he built 4 works machines for Auriol, Fenouil, Loiseaux and himself. Auriol gained his second overall victory and, as the oldest competitor Schek competed as well. One year later he built another 4 machines, with which Rahier and Auriol gained a double victory, Loiseaux was fifth and Schek had his greatest personal success, winning the amateur classification.

As a result of these early successes for the heavyweight offroad bikes with the powerful horizontally-opposed twin motor, HPN was appointed to build the works machines for the Paris-Dakar. A cigarette manufacturer with red house colours had joined the team as the main sponsor. The man in the red and white jacket standing next to the Marlboro-BMW in group photo, Eddy Hau, had joined the team in Paris as a rider besides Rahier and Loizeaux. In 1986 he finished in eigth position on this machine. At the end of the season, the factory withdrew from the Rally provisionally but Hau competed two years later on a private machine, which was also built by HPN and won the Marathon class.

A second machine to be presented at the reunion, was the brainchild of Team Manager Berthold Hauser, the man in the blue team shirt. With the blue *Gauloises* R 900 RR, BMW returned after a 14-year break with a boxer twin through the desert sand and came in third with Lewis as rider. It was also this machine, which was the last BMW works bike to finish the Paris-Dakar in 2001. Since then, HPN's reputation as Dakar bikesmiths has become legendary. Now, even private commissions are no longer accepted by the two gents because this chapter will be closed forever in a few years' time when retirement becomes the order of the day. How great, that these old heroes gather round their former mounts at HPN's former Inn on this grey winter's day and bring them with their reminiscences to light up.

Growing up in a Bavarian village where the annual hillclimb competition started his passion for everything two-wheeled Hermann had his first ride in age of five on a 1930ies Sachs Presto before he ended up wrenching, riding and racing on his pre-electronic Ducatis. He also is head of the organizing committee of the revival hillclimb in his home village. Now living in Munich he is running a marketing and design office, writing and shooting for international motorcycle- and lifestyle-magazines as well as for corporate commissions and is one of the two publishers of BRUMMM.

In einem ehemaligen Gasthaus eines 300 Seelen-Dorfes in der südöstlichen Ecke Bayerns haben Anfang der achziger Jahre Alfred Halbfeld, Klaus Pepperl und Michael Neher ihr Basislager aufgeschlagen und bauen seither im früheren Pferdestall reinrassige Geländemaschinen auf. Das *N* im Firmenname *HPN Motorradtechnik* ist zwar nach ein paar Jahren wieder ausgestiegen, aber das was Halbfeld und Pepperl von dort aus produzieren, ist unter Fans der weißblauen Marke zu Kultstatus gelangt. Ihre Lager, Garagen und der kleine Ausstellungsraum sind vollgestopft mit feinsten Ersatzteilen und mit Motorrädern, die Geschichte geschrieben haben.

Es ist ein verregneter Wintertag, als sich an diesem geschichtsträchtigen Ort ein paar ergraute Herren zu einem Wiedersehen treffen. Viele Jahre sind seither vergangen, aber als sie sich im Innenhof begrüßen und – wie es alte Freunde nun mal tun – von ihren gemeinsamen Erlebnissen erzählen, lauscht man fast andächtig ihren Erzählungen ruhmreicher Zeiten.

Ein Herr in der Runde, Laszlo Peres, war bereits vor den prestigeträchtigen Paris-Dakar-Erfolgen eine treibende Kraft in der Entwicklung von Geländesportmaschinen des Münchener Herstellers. Als nämlich in der deutschen Meisterschaft 1977 eine Geländesportklasse für Fahrzeuge mit mehr als 750 ccm Hubraum eingeführt wurde, baute er mit zwei Kollegen in der Versuchsabteilung von BMW die Six Days GS mit einem Trockengewicht von nur 124 Kilogramm auf, mit der er im Folgejahr sogar als Amateurfahrer Vizemeister wurde.

1979 wurde die legendäre Rallye Paris-Dakar ins Leben gerufen und bereits zum zweiten Veranstaltungsjahr waren die Bayern mit eigenem Boxer-Team am Start. Dietmar Beinhauer, einer der heutigen Gäste des Hauses HPN an diesem Nachmittag, war seinerzeit Teamchef, baute die ersten *Les Concessionnaires* Maschinen noch mit einem Bekannten in dessen Werkstatt zuhause auf und verhalf seinem Arbeitgeber mit den Fahrern Auriol und Fenouil zu großem Ansehen, als Auriol auf der *LePoint* 1981 den ersten Gesamtsieg einfuhr.

Ein anderer, aus dem Allgäu angereister Gast, ist 14-mal deutscher Gelände- und zweifacher Europameister gewesen, holte 12-mal bei den Six Days Weltmeisterschaften Gold, und nachdem er nach dem Reglement nach 25 Jahren Teilnahme für zu alt befunden wurde, fuhr er noch anschließend 15-mal von Paris nach Dakar. Mit 84 Jahren geht der charismatische Heribert Schek heute immer noch bei Klassik-Endurofahrten an den Start und belebt die Veranstaltungen mit seiner Anwesenheit. Er baute 1983 vier Werksmaschinen auf, für Auriol, Fenouil, Loizeaux und für sich selbst. Auriol holte mit der *LePoint-BMW* seinen zweiten Gesamtsieg und Schek fuhr mit 49 Jahren als ältester Teilnehmer natürlich auch selbst mit. Das Jahr darauf baute er erneut vier Maschinen auf, mit denen Rahier und Auriol den Doppelsieg einfuhren, Loizeaux Fünfter wurde und Schek mit dem Sieg in der Amateurwertung seinen persönlich größten Erfolg erzielte.

Nach diesen ersten Erfolgen der schweren Geländemaschinen mit dem starken Boxermotor wurde schließlich HPN damit beauftragt, die Werksrenner für Paris-Dakar aufzubauen. Ein rotfarbiger Zigarettenhersteller war als Hauptsponsor eingestiegen, neben Rahier und Loizeaux war der Mann in der rot-weissen Jacke auf dem Gruppenfoto um die Marlboro-BMW herum, Eddy Hau, als Fahrer an die Pariser Startlinie gegangen. 1986 belegte auf dieser Maschine den achten Rang. Nach der Saison stieg das Werk vorläufig aus der Rallye aus, aber Hau fuhr zwei Jahre später auf einer privaten und ebenfalls von HPN aufgebauten Maschine den Sieg in der Marathonwertung ein.

Eine weitere Maschine, die zum Klassentreffen auf den Hof geschoben wird, wurde von Berthold Hauser, dem Mann im blauen Teamhemd, als Teamchef verantwortet. Mit der *blauen Gauloises* R 900 RR fuhr BMW nach 14 Jahren Pause wieder auf einem Boxer durch den Wüstensand und holte mit Lewis am Lenker den dritten Platz. Diese Maschine war es auch, die zum letzten Mal im Jahre 2001 als Werksmaschine für BMW in Dakar einfuhr. Seither ist HPN's Geschichte als Dakar-Bike-Schmiede zur Legende herangewachsen. Selbst private Aufträge nehmen die beiden Herren keine mehr an, denn in ein paar Jahren soll das Kapitel endgültig geschlossen und in Rente gegangen werden. Wie schön, dass das Gasthaus HPN an diesem grauen Wintertag die alten Helden um ihre einstigen Fahrzeuge versammeln konnte, sie mit ihren Geschichten zum Leuchten brachten.

Aufgewachsen in einem kleinen bayerischen Ort, in dem die jährlichen Bergrennen schon früh seine Zweirad-Leidenschaft weckten, ist er mit fünf Jahren zum ersten Mal auf einer 1930er Sachs Presto gefahren, schraubt und fährt mittlerweile am liebsten alte Ducatis und ist Vorstand eines Vereins, der das ehemalige Bergrennen wieder als Oldtimer-Veranstaltung in seinem Heimatort aufleben lässt. Er lebt in München, führt eine kleine Marketing- und Design-Agentur, schreibt und fotografiert sowohl für verschiedene internationale Lifestyle- und Motorradmagazine als auch Firmenkunden und ist einer der beiden Herausgeber von BRUMMM.

www.hermannkoepf.com

BRUMMM

Photographers in Second Edition
Dimitri Coste
Christian Eusterhus
Kristina Fender
Hermann Köpf
Hiroyuki Maeda
Larry Niehues
James Tyler Reed
Ferruccio Testi (1882–1958)
Mick Woollett (1930–2014)

For more information about retailers, shops and next issues please visit:
www.brummm.com

Creative Direction
Hermann Köpf hk@brummm.com
Christian Eusterhus ce@brummm.com

Artdirection
Nikolaus Hurlbrink
www.nik.is

Postproduction
Ralf Schneider
www.ralf-schneider-retouching.com

Print Production
Eusterhus Druck GmbH
Dieselstraße 26
33442 Herzebrock-Clarholz, Germany
www.eusterhusdruck.de

Illustration
Nicolai Sclater aka Ornamental Conifer
@ornamentalconifer

Thanks to
Danny Eales, Maximilian Funk,
Jochen Kleine, Stefan Knittel,
Tadashi Kono, Dieter Mutschler,
Christoph Wilhelm

Publisher
Hermann Köpf & Christian Eusterhus
Kader Eins GmbH
Thierschstrasse 25
80538 Munich, Germany
www.kadereins.net

Distributed by
gestalten

sales@gestalten.com
www.gestalten.com

© BRUMMM 2017
– including all content are protected by copyright law.

Order-Number: BRU0217197569